FOREIGN DIRECT INVESTMENT AND URBAN GROWTH IN CHINA

Foreign Direct Investment and Urban Growth in China

LEI WANG

Wuhan University, China
and
Peking University, China

Routledge
Taylor & Francis Group

LONDON AND NEW YORK

First published 2011 by Ashgate Publishing

2 Park Square, Milton Park, Abingdon, Oxon OX14 4RN
711 Third Avenue, New York, NY 10017, USA

Routledge is an imprint of the Taylor & Francis Group, an informa business

First issued in paperback 2016

British Library Cataloguing in Publication Data
Wang, Lei.
    Foreign direct investment and urban growth in China.
    1. Investments, Foreign–China–History–20th century. 2. Investments, Foreign–China–History–21st century. 3. City planning–China–History–20th century. 4. City planning–China–History–21st century. 5. Cities and towns–Growth–Economic aspects–China–History–20th century. 6. Cities and towns–Growth–Economic aspects–China–History–21st century. 7. Real estate development–China–History–20th century. 8. Real estate development–China–History–21st century.
    I. Title
    307.1'216'0951–dc22

Library of Congress Cataloging-in-Publication Data
Wang, Lei, 1977–
    Foreign direct investment and urban growth in China / by Lei Wang.
       p. cm.
    Includes bibliographical references and index.
    ISBN 978-1-4094-0685-3 (hardback : alk. paper)
    1. Investments, Foreign–China. 2. China–Economic conditions. 3. New business enterprises–China. 4. Economic development–China. I. Title.

HG5782.W3617 2011
332.67'30951–dc22

                                                                                      2010053052

ISBN 978-1-4094-0685-3 (hbk)
ISBN 978-1-138-26081-8 (pbk)

Contents

List of Figures

List of Tables

Abbreviations

BVIs	British Virgin Islands
CBD	Central Business District
CBRC	China Banking Regulatory Commission
CCP	Chinese Communist Party
CCPCC	Chinese Communist Party Central Committee
CCTV	China Central Television
CEOA	Coastal Economic Open Areas
CI	Cayman Islands
CJC	Contractual Joint Venture
CKD	Complete Knocked Down
CNS	China News Service
COC	Coastal Open City
CSRC	China Securities Regulatory Commission
EJC	Equity Joint Venture
EIT	Enterprise Income Tax
ETDZ	Economic and Technological Development Zone
FAR	Floor Area Ratio
FDI	Foreign Direct Investment
FIE	Foreign Invested Enterprise
GAC	General Administration of Customs
GDP	Gross Domestic Product
IMF	International Monetary Fund
IPO	Initial Public Offering
JV	Joint Venture
LTB	Local Taxation Bureau
LURs	Land Use Rights
MLR	Ministry of Land and Resources
MNC	Multi-National Corporation
M&A	Merger and Acquisition
MOF	Ministry of Finance
MOC	Ministry of Commerce
NAO	National Audit Office
NDRC	National Development and Reform Commission
NPC	National People's Congress
NTB	National Taxation Bureau
OECD	Organisation for Economic Co-operation and Development
OFI	Other Foreign Investment
OC	Open City

PA	Processing and Assembly
PBC	People's Bank of China
PRC	People's Republic of China
QFII	Qualified Foreign Institutional Investors
RMB	Ren Min Bi (Chinese currency)
SAFE	State Administration of Foreign Exchange
SAIC	State Administration for Industry and Commerce
SEZ	Special Economic Zone
SKD	Semi-Knocked Down
SOE	State-Owned Enterprise
SSB	State Statistical Bureau
TRIM	Trade-Related Investment Measures
UNCTAD	United Nations Conference on Trade and Development
US	United States
VAT	Value-Added Tax
WFOE	Wholly Foreign-Owned Enterprise
WTO	World Trade Organization

Acknowledgements

This book originates from the recognition that China's path of transformation notably represented in its urban settings largely results from the interaction of global and domestic forces. The development of such a perspective is built upon both theoretical inquiries and empirical investigations that would not be possible without the spiritual, intellectual and physical support from a wide range of individuals and institutions. My greatest debt is to my parents who have been in support of my efforts with virtually everything they have, to my wife, Yin, who has been with me with her deep love, and to my child, Jason, whose arrival to this world brings me tremendous joys.

I am grateful to have received education and affection from incredible teachers and mentors I came across as a student, among whom Xinmu Wu initially inspired me to work in this area and Elliott Sclar have had the greatest impact on my thinking. Xiaoling Wei has taught me more than I could ever have imagined about life philosophy. Lan Yao has been a particularly great teacher for my English language. Susan Fainstein broadened my understanding of social science studies and Smita Srinivas offered a great deal of help with regard to literature reading and academic writing. Carl Riskin informed me of Chinese political economy through his well-delivered lectures and provided invaluable input to the framework of my research. Yiu Por Chen and Clara Irazábel raised their thought-provoking comments on methodology.

I have been very fortunate in having colleagues with whom to conduct research work for this book. Yin Zhu, Wei Wang, Zhigang Li, Xianghua Liu and Zhigao Liu provided critical assistance to field surveys and data collection across different places. Discussions with Minquan Liu and engagement with the Center for Human and Economic Development Studies (CHEDS) under his directorship as a Research Fellow helped illuminate the role of land in joining domestic and global forces and shaping urban physical and economic development. Hongwei Dong and Yunjing Li have been insightful and amazing collaborators in a few projects this book is based on.

I also benefited from generous funding as well as accommodating institutional settings to go through the whole process of intellectual exploration. The extensive fieldwork and data collection in the initial stage of investigation can hardly be conducted in a financially smooth way without the aid of quite a few grants and fellowships from Columbia University's Weatherhead East Asian Institute. The conference travel to present this research publicly and intensive revision work based on feedback were supported by "the Fundamental Research Funds for the Central Universities" in China, and the final publication project is sponsored by "the Scientific Research Foundation for Returned Overseas Chinese Scholars,

State Education Ministry" of China. I thank Jianqing Zhang and other colleagues at Wuhan University's Institute for the Development of Central China (IDCC), with which I am currently affiliated, for their efforts to provide me a supportive environment where I can complete this research with dedication. I think the birth of this book would be the best return to everyone who kindly extended to me their tangible support and encouragement.

Introduction

It is argued that one of the great transformations of economic systems in the twentieth century was the transition from a centrally planned system to a market-based one, in which China is being heralded as a case deserving special interest (Qian, 2006). For almost three decades since 1978, China has maintained an average annual growth rate of gross domestic product (GDP) around 10 percent, making it one of the most rapidly growing economies in the world. There is little doubt that China's economic successes are associated with "decentralization, marketization and globalization" (Wei, 2000). According to Nicolas Lardy (Lardy, 1994), China is more fully integrated with the world economy than was South Korean or Taiwan at a comparable stage of development. A more recent research suggests that China now has a far more open economy than Japan in the sense that its trade in 2004 was equal to 70 percent of its GDP, in contrast to Japan's 24 percent, and it received US$60.6 billion in foreign direct investment (FDI) while Japan received US$20.1 billion (Overholt, 2005).[1]

Indeed, the magnitude of FDI flow into China is so impressive that few could ignore its significance to the Chinese economy. Since 1978 when China opened its door to the rest of the world, the amounts of contracted and utilized FDI inflows have been increasing all the way from negligible levels to US$200.17 billion and US$69.47 billion in 2006 respectively (see Figure 1.1).[2] These FDI inflows are anchored at 274.9 thousand direct investment enterprises, or "foreign invested enterprises" (FIEs), across 30 provincial regions. During the past three decades, China has been committed US$1285.7 billion FDI in which a cumulative total of US$622.4 billion has been actually utilized. According to the United Nations Conference on Trade and Development (UNCTAD) statistics, China has been the world's largest recipient country of FDI in the developing world and was second only to the United States during the many years in the 1990s and first decade of the twenty-first century (UNCTAD, 2008).

---

1   As commonly understood, China's inward FDI includes those cross-border investments originating from Hong Kong, Macau and Taiwan.

2   Contracted FDI is the FDI that is signed into investment contracts. Utilized FDI is the FDI that the host country has actually received in a certain year. For a given project, the contracted investment is usually distributed across years. Generally a function of contracted FDI in the adjacent previous years, utilized FDI is more appropriate to examine the factual impacts on host economy while the contractual is useful to represent the demand of host economy or willingness of investors, or both.

Measuring FDI

The aim of this reseach is to examine the causes that give rise to the pattern of FDI in China. The grand picture presented above on the basis of aggregate statistics, however, needs to be re-examined against the size of the host country in order to understand the extent to which FDI is involved in Chinese economy or the particular significance FDI inflows have for the economic growth of China. The reason is other things equal, a larger economy is supposed to receive more FDI than a smaller one can. That is to say, higher FDI inflows of a certain country may just be the outcome of the larger size of its economy and FDI inflow figures that demonstrate an increasing pattern over time may simply result from the growing economy of the host country.

Taking that relative issue into consideration, indicators that are frequently used to measure the pattern of FDI in its host economy include the "ratio of FDI to fixed asset investments," the "ratio of FDI to GDP," the "ratio of industrial output value of FIEs to total industrial output values," the "ratio of taxes collected from FIEs to those collected from all firms" and the "ratio of exports by FIEs to total national exports." The first two address the significance of FDI directly while the other

Table I.1   The ratios of industrial output, tax contribution and export of FIEs to those of all enterprises, 1990–2006 (%)

	Output ratio	Tax ratio	Export ratio
1992	7.09	4.25	20.44
1993	9.15	5.71	27.51
1994	11.26	8.51	28.69
1995	14.31	10.96	31.51
1996	15.14	11.87	40.71
1997	18.57	13.16	41.00
1998	24.00	14.38	44.06
1999	27.75	15.99	45.47
2000	22.51	17.50	47.93
2001	28.05	19.01	50.06
2002	33.37	20.52	52.20
2003	35.87	20.86	54.83
2004	31.43	20.81	57.06
2005	31.41	20.71	58.30
2006	31.50	21.19	58.18

Note: "Output ratio," "tax ratio" and "export ratio" refer to the "ratio of industrial output value of FIEs to total industrial output values"; the "ratio of taxes collected from FIEs to those collected from all firms" and the "ratio of exports by FIEs to total national exports" respectively.

Source: *China Commerce Yearbook*, various years.

three reflect that of FIEs, in which FDI sometimes partner with Chinese domestic capital to form a joint venture.[3]

This book chooses the "ratio of FDI to fixed asset investments" (abbreviated as "investment index" hereafter) to represent the significance of FDI inflows for the host country. Although the FIE-based indicators clearly demonstrate their increasing weight in Chinese economy (see Table I.1), it is difficult to single out the contributions of FDI to that firm-level performance, which is the focus of investigation here. Besides, the incomplete official statistics on sector-based GDP makes it technically impossible to assess the distinct dynamics of FDI across industries by computing the "ratio of FDI to GDP" for individual sectors.

As the result of magnitude of utilized FDI inflows in a certain year divided by the total fixed asset investments made by all entities during that same period, "investment index" are no longer plagued by the same problems as associated with the other indicators. But two important factors may affect its effectiveness to reflect the overall pattern of FDI in its host economy. The first one is the modal distribution of FDI. According to International Monetary Fund (IMF) and Organisation for Economic Cooperation and Development (OECD) countries (IMF 2008; OECD 2008), FDI refers only to the investment that aims to possess or acquire a "lasting interest" or have an "effective voice" in the management of the foreign enterprise, which is defined as holding no less than 10 per cent of ordinary shares or voting power of the direct investment enterprise. Under this definition, a majority of FDI inflows in most developed countries are those international financial transactions on the stock market that acquires 10 percent or more voting power of an enterprise, or cross-border mergers and acquisitions (M&As).

In contrast, most FDI inflows in developing countries are greenfield investments financing equipments and plant investments rather than acquiring existing assets via stock market that are not well-functioning or even absent at all in many cases there. In addition, some regulations against substantive foreign control of domestic enterprises through equity acquisition also contribute to the the lack of foreign acquisition of shares from the stock market. China, for example, set two separate stock markets, namely A-share and B-share markets, in the early 1990s for domestic and foreign investors respectively with the intention to keep the nascent stock market from the manipulation of international capital. Due to the limited shares circulating on the B-share market, however, it is difficult for foreign investors to hold more than 25 percent of an issuing firm's entire equity. When the

---

3 According to Chinese official definition, FIEs are basically divided into three types that are equity joint ventures (EJVs), contractual joint ventures (CJVs) and wholly foreign-owned enterprises (WFOEs). As the major form of FDI, an EJV is an independent registered limited liability company capitalized by foreign and Chinese domestic funds, while a WFOE is one with capital solely contributed by the foreign investor. A CJV is similar to EJV in many aspects except the former does not have to be a separate legal person and the distribution of control, risks and profits among parties are subject to contract terms rather than the capital they invest.

A-share market became open to Qualified Foreign Institutional Investors (QFIIs) and foreign strategic investors in 2002, it is still regulated that the proportion of shares owned by QFIIs and foreign strategic investors may not exceed 20 and 25 percent for an issuing firm in any industries and one in financial sector respectively (CSRC,2006). Although foreign strategic investors are allowed to acquire any amount of shares of a non-financial issuing firm, those cases with higher than 25 percent of voting power are still rare because of the substantial non-circulating shares owned by the state.

Besides, the practice of financial accounting in China sets 25 percent, a threshold higher than that of IMF and OECD, as the minimum equity share for international capital inflows to be classified as FDI and the direct investment enterprise to be eligible for preferential policy treatments (NPC, 1979). According to this more stringent criterion, foreign purchases of the listed companies' equity shares on the stock markets of Shanghai and Shenzhen that reach the 25 percent line and can be classified as FDI are even fewer.

The different combination of these two FDI modes between developing and developed worlds suggests "investment index" be adjusted so that it can be internationally comparable. The numerator in the formula of "investment index" includes FDI in both modes where greenfield FDI are material production on the basis of newly created fixed assets that usually generates immediate impact on the host economy, while M&As are to transfer the ownership of a firm's assets that affects the host economy only in a much more sophisticated and moderate fashion. As a result, the "investment index" may overestimate the significance of FDI for their host economies, with greater bias for countries that have higher proportions of M&As than for those otherwise.

The second factor that may affect the effectiveness of "investment index" is the scale of analysis. The aggregate indicator for the whole economy may not reflect the dynamics of FDI in individual sectors that may differ widely from one another. Two reasons account for that variance across sectors. One is the highly uneven sectoral distribution of FDI. By the end of 2006, more than 60 percent accumulative FDI inflows have been contracted in Chinese manufacturing industry, which is followed by the sector of real estate that has accommodated 16.24 percent of the total contracted FDI. The other is that different sectors are usually characterized by rather distinct capital composition. For example, real estate sector usually have a higher content of domestic capital than manufacturing for the sake of its territorial nature. Considerable difference would then be expected between the investment indices computed for these two broad sectors, which means the overall "investment index" could be an inaccurate or even misleading indicator of FDI dynamics for a particular sector of interest.

The quantitative significance of FDI for its host economies as reflected by "investment index" is just one aspect of the FDI pattern that needs to be identified. This book also uses the average size of projects capitalized by FDI (called "size index" hereafter), or the value of the contracted FDI inflows divided by the number of projects they commit to capitalize, to mirror the general qualitative condition of FDI inflows. The reason that "size index" may stand proxy for the quality of FDI is related to round-tripping FDI in China that refers to capital of Chinese origin moving offshore first and then coming back as FDI to capture the policy benefits exclusively offered to FIEs. As investing abroad will inevitably incur greater cultural, managerial or physical costs than domestically, FIEs funded by capital from abroad must have some advantages over their domestic rivals in brand names, management and marketing skills, proprietary technology, financial strength, or economies of scale, which the round-tripping FDI does not have to possess given their origin in China. Such round-tripping capital is usually characterized by small scale and low content of technological and managerial skills. Thus, a constantly increasing "size index" may suggest the declining share of such round-tripping capital in the pool of FDI inflows as well as the improved overall quality of projects capitalized by FDI, which will be more systematically tested in the first chapter of this book.

Structure of the Book

This book argues the dynamics of FDI inflows in China as identified on the basis of "investment index" and "size index" results from the entrepreneurial orientation of local states to maximize short-term economic and revenue growth. It is organized in five chapters to illustrate the pattern of FDI as well as its underlying political economic foundation, facilitating institutional mechanisms and social consequences. Particularly, Chapter 1 investigates the course of FDI in China and computes the "investment index" and "size index." It shows the mid 1990s and the years since the start of this century are the two periods with surging FDI inflows, unparalleled "investment index" and rising "size index," which can hardly be captured by conventional theories on the location choice of FDI. In order to provide a convincing account of the FDI pattern as identified, this book incorporates China's domestic demand-side factors that favor manufacturing FDI over domestic capital into the analytical framework.

Chapter 2 starts with the key parameters of Chinese local state entrepreneurialism and investigates the political economic motivations underlying it. It shows Chinese local states heavily depend on the growing sectors of manufacturing and real estate as their major sources of revenues, which distinguish the China's local state entrepreneurialism from both the "entrepreneurialism" in the Schumpeterian sense and the conventional orientation of developmental state. One of the reasons for the rise of such local state entrepreneurialism is the centralized political system that strongly motivates local officials to maximize the tangible achievements within their office terms and usually leads to the quantitative growth of these two sectors. The other is the economic incentives arising from the fiscal arrangements between the central and local governments. By focusing on the decentralized and re-centralized systems before and after 1994, this chapter finds the scheme established that year not only made FIEs the key agent in place of state-owned enterprises (SOEs) to achieve local economic and revenue growth, which resulted in the influx of FDI, rocketing "investment index" and rising "size index" in the mid 1990s, it also institutionalized the significance of real estate and manufacturing sectors for local economic and revenue growth.

Motivated by the political and fiscal systems of China, the rise of entrepreneurial local states in China is further facilitated by the urban housing and land use reforms initiated at the end of last century. The following two chapters deal with the land-based strategies of Chinese local states to materialize the entrepreneurial projects and their resulted preferences for manufacturing FDI over domestic capital, which contributes to the wave of FDI inflows as observed in the early 2000s. Specifically, Chapter 3 reveals how Chinese local states that are the *de facto* owners of urban land tried to drive up the price of land used for residential and commercial development by limiting its supply and allowing higher floor-area ratios. On the other hand, Chapter 4 shows how the municipalities managed to maintain exceedingly low prices of land for manufacturing production in order to encourage inward investment. The contrasting pricing strategies for different land uses prompted relentless acquisition of arable land by municipalities on the one hand and implied high direct and opportunity costs associated with manufacturing uses on the other. With land resource becoming an increasingly tight constraint against rampant urban economic and physical growth, localities have greater demand for manufacturing FDI that is generally more land-efficient as will be demonstrated in the second half of this chapter.

Chapter 5 presents the regional variance of local state entrepreneurialism across eastern, middle and western China. Overall, eastern region has a stronger motivation to expedite local economic growth than hinterland as a much higher proportion of their local revenues were financed by their own efforts to mobilize revenue collection. That is materialized by the more contrasting land pricing in eastern cities. The ratios between land prices for residential and commercial uses and those for manufacturing uses were greater in the coastal regions than elsewhere. As a result of the more finite land resource and more entrepreneurial land-based strategies, the significance of FDI for local economies, as reflected by the "investment index," is greater in the east accordingly. That regional comparison, however, does not mean no changes at all in the hinterland over time. Rather, places in middle and western China are also demonstrating increasingly stronger local state entrepreneurialism as measured by the same set of indicators.

This book concludes with policy implications for sustainable urban development. The current land-based urban economic and spatial growth in China generates multi-fold peril. As the soaring residential land and housing prices are well beyond the affordability of regular urban households, the housing market is increasingly subject to the manipulation of speculation capital and deviates from its social function. Preference for FDI over domestic industrial investment as a result of such land-based growth strategies puts the latter at asymmetric disadvantage and may cause economic imbalance. Besides, the pattern that urban economic and spatial growth heavily depends on exogenous investment and export rather than endogenous innovation can hardly be sustained environmentally. These call for reforms in land use regulations and the fiscal system and greater political accountability to make urban development in China more harmonious, balanced and sustainable.

On Sources

The preliminary idea of this book was shaped in study tours in winter 2005 and in summer 2007. The first was in the development zones of Dalian, Linyi, Xiamen and Guangzhou, which are four major cities located in the four coastal provinces of Liaoning, Shandong, Fujian and Guangdong respectively. The second was conducted at the hinterland cities of Wuhan and Nanjing and was more intensive with face-to-face interaction with government officials in charge of foreign investments and land-use planning as well as enterprise managers of FIEs. Although these field experiences rarely produced systematic data that can be directly put into quantitative analysis, they deeply impressed me with the entrepreneurial orientation of Chinese local states and gave me a critical sense of the role that land use plays in urban physical and economic growth, which eventually guides me through the formulation of research questions and the development of methodology.

This book extensively draws upon statistics published by Chinese statistical authorities for quantitative analysis. The principal sources for FDI statistics include *China Statistical Yearbook*, *China Commerce Yearbook*, *China Foreign Economic Statistical Yearbook* and *Almanac of China's Foreign Economic Relations and Trade*. For statistics on public finance, land use and industries, *Finance Yearbook of China*, *China Land and Resources Almanac* and *China Industry Economy Statistical Yearbook* are the main references. In addition to these official statistical yearbooks, some quantitative data and qualitative evidence are also collected from a wide range of other sources such as government documents, journal articles, online databases and media reports.

Perhaps the biggest concern with those quantitative sources that are used throughout this book is their reliability. The functional departments of Chinese local governments are usually responsible for collecting and reporting statistics of the particular sphere they are in charge of. That organizational practice may cause conflict of interest and result in inflated numbers that can be used to highlight the performances achieved under their administration. My research findings, however, would seem to be tenable in front of that risk not only because they can be supported by qualitative evidence, but also because most statistics that are frequently cited in this book are ratio-based indicators. Even though some numbers are tampered with, it is very unlikely that the manipulation could happen on such a large scale or in such a sophisticated way that the ratios between them would be systematically distorted as well, for the data compilers are not aware of the question this book is going to address. Besides, not all statistics are equally easy to manipulate. For example, data on fiscal revenues and expenditures has to be consistent with the money actually collected and dispensed and is believed to be more credible than that which is unilaterally reported by authorities.

Chapter 1

Toward a Demand-Side Perspective for FDI Dynamics in China

Since China explicitly stated its policy orientation toward reform and openness in the late 1970s, FDI has been present in this country for over three decades. The path of its evolution with it ups and downs, however, is not a linear process. In order to clarify the pattern of FDI as the object of this book's inquiry, this chapter begins from the qualitative review of its history in China and divides the past into four periods in which FDI dynamic was most vibrant in the early 1990s and early 2000s. In addition to the surging magnitude of inflows, further analysis of "investment index" and "size index" in the second section of this chapter shows FDI had been significant in Chinese manufacturing industries during those two periods and it tended to capitalize larger projects with higher content of management and technological skills. The final section of this chapter attempts to uncover the forces underlying this pattern through conventional theoretical views that focus on FDI itself almost exclusively. Their unsatisfactory explanatory power, however, prompts a demand-side perspective that will be elaborated throughout the rest of this book.

1.1 History of FDI in China

According to the fluctuating magnitude of contracted inflows, the trajectory of FDI in China can be divided into four periods: 1979–1991, 1992–1993, 1994–1999 and 2000–date (see Figure 1.1). Although the first FIE in China was established in 1979, there had been pretty few FDI during the whole 1980s. The impressive significance of FDI in China is only a relatively recent phenomenon that occurred as late as 1992. Immediately following its doubled growth in the brief two-year period, the inflows plummeted as a result of stringent state regulations and its revival had not been observed until the beginning of this century. By tracing the co-evolution between this cross-border capital flow and China's domestic policies, the historical account in this section provides contextual basis for further inquiries hereafter.

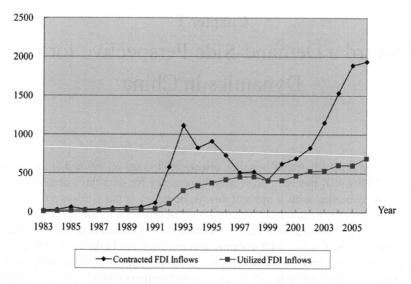

Figure 1.1   Contracted and utilized FDI inflows, 1983–2006 (in US$ 100 millions)

Source: *China Statistical Yearbook*, various years.

1.1.1 Period One: 1979–1991

FDI in China can be dated back to 1979 when the Gang of Four was smashed and new leadership endorsed the general program of reforms and opening on the 3rd Plenary Session of the 11th Party Congress. In July of that year, the Law of the PRC on Chinese–Foreign Equity Joint Ventures was promulgated, which officially announced the reversal of China's policy standing of autarky that had been dominating Maoist period (NPC, 1979). To attract FDI that was imminently needed to the capital construction of China, the Income Tax Law of the PRC on Chinese–Foreign Equity Joint Ventures of 1980 offered joint venture 30 percent tax rate, or an effective rate of 33 percent when an 10 percent local surcharge on the accessed income tax is included, on its income from which "the costs, expenses and losses have been deducted" (NPC, 1980). This was more than 20 percent lower than the income tax rate for state-owned large- and medium-sized enterprises that had had to turn in 55 percent of their income to the state until 1994.[1] In addition, joint ventures scheduled to operate for 10 years or more were

---

1   SOEs had been required to turn in all of their profits to the state without any tax liabilities before 1 June 1983. After that, large- and medium-sized SOEs started to pay a flat tax of 55 percent on their income from 1 June of 1983. They were also required to remit a portion of their post-tax profits to the state. Small SOEs should pay tax on an eight-level

exempt from income tax in the first two profit-making years, and allowed a 50 percent reduction in the three following years.

In the meanwhile, special institutional and policy arrangements were offered to some coastal regions to attract investments, promote export and test reform initiatives. In 1980 four "Special Economic Zones" (SEZs) were established in China's southeast with enormously preferential policies. Zhuhai, Shenzhen, Shantou, all in Guangdong Province, and Xiamen in Fujian Province were situated close to the capitalist economies of Macao, Hong Kong, and Taiwan. In 1984, 14 more "Coastal Open Cities" (COCs) were given preferential policies comparable to those at SEZs. FIEs operating within the boundary of Economic and Technological Development Zones (ETDZs) of these cities were eligible for the same enterprise income tax (EIT) rate of flat 15 percent as those located in SEZs. This was much lower than the 30 percent income tax rate for joint ventures in the rest of the country.

Besides, foreign investors whose firms are located in both SEZs and the ETDZs of COCs were allowed to repatriate profits abroad without being subject to any additional tax that had to be levied in other places. Local governments in these regions were authorized to exempt local surcharges on FIEs at their own discretion too (State Council, 1984). In 1985, the Chinese government designated the Pearl River Delta, the Yangtze River Delta and Southern Fujian Delta as "Coastal Economic Open Areas" (CEOAs) that received policy treatments similar to those effective at COCs. In March 1988, the status of CEOAs was further granted to Shandong Peninsula and Liaoning Peninsula. Thus, most areas in the coastal provinces of Liaoning, Shandong, Jiangsu, Zhejiang, Fujian, Guangdong and Guangxi were incorporated into the coverage of CEOAs. In that same year, Hainan Island was elevated to provincial level and became the fifth SEZ.

1.1.2 Period Two: 1992–1993

The initiatives of opening China to the outside world did not stop. Even the Tiananmen Square incident of June 1989 that caused widespread doubt among foreign investors over China's standing on openness and reform did not shift

---

progressive basis ranging from 7 to 55 percent. From October 1st of 1984, the second-step "tax-for-profits" reform stipulated a gradual switch from the co-existence of tax payment and profits remittance to complete substitution of tax payment for profits delivery. See Provisional Regulation Concerning the Tax-for-Profits in SOEs (State Council, 1983) for details. In 1994 when a new round of comprehensive fiscal and tax reform started, the profits of all domestic firms became subject to a flat income tax rate of 33 percent which was still much higher than the 15 percent income tax rate for most FIEs that were located in the special zones as will be explained below. Even the new uniform tax rate of 25 percent effective from 1 January 2008 for all firms, regardless of their nature of ownership, still granted a 5-year transition period to FIEs under preferential tax rate, which will be maintaining tax rate gap between domestic and FIEs before 2013.

this fast-marching giant away from its ongoing path. China's commitment to openness was validated by its decision in 1990 to open and develop the Pudong area of Shanghai. Apart from its significance in reconfirming policy consistency, that decision also marked the switch of policy orientation from merely extending geographical coverage of open areas to deepening the content of opening-up. One of the chief features which distinguish the development of Pudong from that of SEZs or other special zones is the liberalization of FDI in advanced service industries of banking, real estate and business consulting. That generated enormous model effects. Many other provinces requested that the restriction on FDI in banking be relaxed. By the end of 1993, 76 foreign banks and financial institutions with the total asset of US$8.9 billion had been allowed to establish branches in 13 major cities in China (CBRC, 2007). Besides, the transfer of rights of use for state-owned land was also allowed to foreign investors in all SEZs, COCs and CEOAs including Pudong (State Council, 1990a), which symbolized another important shift in China's FDI regime.

With more and more multinational corporations (MNCs) entering China since the opening of Pudong, their demand to establish WFOEs became greater. Also stronger was their objection to the differential tax regimes for foreign-invested joint ventures and WFOEs. Few tax concessions were offered to WFOEs when the Income Tax Law of the PRC on WFOEs was promulgated in 1982. According to that law, the profits of WFOEs were subject to a progressive tax rate ranging from 20 to 40 percent, which was generally higher than that for EJVs and CJVs. That situation remained intact until 1991 when the PRC Income Tax Law for FIEs and Foreign Enterprises (also known as Unified Tax Law) extended the tax treatment for EJVs to WFOEs as well (NPC, 1991).

The critical event in China's course of opening up happened in 1992. In order to secure the opening orientation against the ideological opposition within the Party that was triggered by the political turmoil of 1989, Deng Xiaoping, the principal architect of China's reform and opening, made his famous Southern Tour between January 18 and February 21 in 1992. In the public speeches delivered during that tour, Deng explicitly articulated that "development is just hard truth" as a serious caution against emerging leftist ideology at that time. These ideas were soon endorsed at the politburo meeting that released the Chinese Communist Party Central Committee (CCPCC) document No. 4 in May. As a prelude to the 14th National Congress of CCP, that meeting and the document of "The CCPCC's opinions on expediting reform, opening wider to the outside world, and working harder to raise the economy to a higher level in a better and quicker way" (*zhong gong zhong yang guan yu jia kuai gai ge, kuo da kai fang, li zheng jing ji geng hao geng kuai de shang yi ge xin tai jie de yi jian*) suggested 5 cities along Yangtze River (four more were added in 1993), 11 capital cities in hinterland areas and 13 cities along China's border line as "open cities" (OCs) with the same policy treatment as those effective at COCs and CEOAs (CCPCC, 1992). In October, the 14th National Congress of CCP formally announced building a "socialist market economy" as the development goal of China, which actually declared the abolition of Chen Yun's "birdcage" model and represented a major breakthrough of orthodox Marxist theory.

Meanwhile, a series of new measures was implemented to attract high quality FDI to China. Examples included the removal of restrictions against FDI in more tertiary sectors such as retail and financial services, road, rail and telecommunications as well as exploitation of coal, oil and other minerals. Designed to boost the growth of FDI in China, all these policies succeed in convincing the whole world of China's firm steps toward openness. Responding to the reaffirmed policy coherence, foreign investments poured in. The willingness of international investors then met the great enthusiasm of local governments for business and investments that was triggered by the impending fiscal reform in 1994 (this will be addressed in section 2.2.2.3 of Chapter 2). Such an overlapping effect was epitomized by the rampant sprawl of "development zones" across China in the early 1990s. There were more than 6,000 development zones established by governments on all levels with an aggregate planned acreage of 15,300,000 square kilometers. That was even wider than 13,400,000 square kilometers of the nationwide urban developed areas at that time (Yu and Zheng, 2003). As a result, contracted FDI inflows reached its historical record of 111.4 billion in 1993, more than the sum over all previous years since 1979.

1.1.3 Period Three: 1994–1999

The outcome of such unusual patterns of land and industrial development was a real estate bubble on one hand and overcapacity of manufacturing production on the other. The central government then stepped on the brakes by applying restrictive policies to cool off the economy, which was the start of the third stage of FDI in China. First of all, proposals to set up development zones had to be examined and approved by the State Council rather than by local governments on any level, as was formerly the case (State Council, 1993). Secondly, policies were aimed at channeling FDI into key areas that were essential to the balanced development of the national economy but away from sectors plagued by overcapacity already. For example, in the automobile industry, foreign investors could not set up new car assembly lines until 1997 and after that any foreign car-makers had to meet the requirement of 60 percent local content. This practice was then extended to a wide range of industries in mid 1995 when the first Guiding Catalogue on Industries for Foreign Investment was promulgated. Rather than universally preferential policies toward FDI, this catalogue provided a comprehensive index of industries where FDI would be encouraged, allowed, restricted or prohibited respectively.

The channeling effort was accompanied by the third major initiative in late 1995, which was the proposed general overhaul of preferential tax policies for all FIEs. Under the old regime, FIEs paid 15 percent EIT in SEZs and in the ETDZs of open cities, 24 percent in the other areas of open cities, and 30 percent elsewhere. This tax system would be replaced by a flat 30 percent national corporate tax. Although this proposal did not come into effect, other measures against FIEs were taken. Tax collection from FIEs was stressed. The preferential customs duty rate on equipments imported by FIEs was aborted. The bank guarantee account system was required for firms engaging in export processing in which FIEs played an important role.

The implementation of all these policies prompted Goldman Sachs and Morgan Stanley to downgrade their ratings of China as a destination country for cross-border investments. Some existing foreign investors withdrew from projects under construction, and prospective foreign investors became hesitant. The immediate consequence was the shrinking of contracted FDI inflows, which was further complicated by the breakout of the Asian financial crisis in 1997. The joint aftermath of domestic austerity and international storm extended into the next few years. In 1999, the contracted FDI inflow was US$ 41.2 billion, only one third of the level attained in 1993.

1.1.4 Period Four: 2000-date

The darkest hour is before dawn, which is also true for the path of FDI in China. When the world economy recovered from financial crisis and the daunting effects of stringent policies faded away, FDI inflows started a new round of upsurge. In 2002, the contracted US$82.8 billion surpassed US$73.3 billion, the magnitude that was achieved in 1996 on the eve of financial crisis. In just one year after that, the historical height of US$111.4 billion which was attained in 1993 was refreshed by the new record of US$115.1 billion. This momentum continued into 2006 when more than US$200 billion FDI was contracted. So did the actually utilized inflow of US$64.4 billion in 1997 which reached US$73.5 billion in 2006 (SSB, various years-a).

The extraordinary FDI inflows, whether measured in contracted or actual utilized term, can hardly be attributed to the recovery of world economy because they were well beyond the height attained before the crisis and few other countries had such an achievement. Neither can it be the outcome of domestic policies toward openness that have not significantly changed since the beginning of this century. In order to uncover the forces underlying FDI dynamics of which absolute magnitude is just one aspect, we now turn to the structural features as will be revealed by "investment index" and "size index," which may help us identify the pattern of FDI and prompt a new perspective.

1.2 "Investment Index" and "Size Index"

As illustrated in the introduction of this book, "investment index" reflects the weight of FDI in relation to domestic investment and "size index" gives us an overall picture of the projects FDI capitalizes. Their effectiveness, however, depends on whether or not the modal and sectoral distributions of FDI are taken into consideration. This section will compute "investment index" for greenfield manufacturing FDI and complement "size index" with the analysis of round-tripping FDI and other cross-border investments in low-skill fields.

1.2.1 High "Investment Index"

It is clear from the UNCTAD statistics of FDI that China had a much higher "investment index" than the world average for most of the years in the 1990s (see Table 1.1). That no longer seems to be the case during the period from 1999 to 2007 when the "investment index" of China was not only lower than that of developed country such as the UK or a developing one like Brazil, but also fell below the world average from time to time. Indeed, literal interpretations developed on the ground of horizontal cross-country comparison and vertical temporal dimension seen in Table 1.1 usually lead to two misleading claims about FDI dynamics in China (Jiang, 2006). One is that FDI in China may not be an important issue deserving special attention because its "investment index" was not as high as that of the UK, Taiwan or Brazil. It was even below the world average for many of the years since the late 1990s. The other is that the "investment index" that has been generally decreasing over time suggests the diminishing significance of FDI to the Chinese economy. That tended to continue without any sign of reversal even when the impacts of the Asian financial crisis had been admittedly mitigated.

Table 1.1   The "investment indices" across countries/regions, 1990–2007 (%)

	China	US	UK	Korea	Taiwan	India	Brazil	World
1990	3.5	4.8	15.0	0.8	3.6	0.3	1.0	4.3
1991	3.8	2.3	8.0	0.9	3.1	0.1	1.5	3.1
1992	7.1	1.9	8.7	0.5	1.7	0.4	2.9	3.1
1993	11.9	4.6	9.8	0.4	1.6	0.8	1.5	4.1
1994	16.8	3.7	5.6	0.5	2.2	1.3	1.9	4.4
1995	15.0	4.5	10.7	0.7	2.3	2.2	3.0	5.3
1996	14.4	6.0	12.4	1.0	2.9	2.6	7.2	5.9
1997	14.4	6.7	15.2	1.4	3.3	3.7	11.8	7.4
1998	13.2	10.4	29.6	4.8	0.3	2.7	18.6	11.0
1999	10.9	15.6	34.7	7.5	4.2	2.0	28.2	16.3
2000	10.0	16.1	48.6	5.7	6.4	3.4	30.3	20.3
2001	10.3	8.2	22.0	2.9	7.3	4.9	23.9	12.3
2002	10.0	4.0	9.2	2.1	2.6	4.6	20.0	9.3
2003	8.3	2.7	5.7	2.4	0.8	3.0	12.0	7.4
2004	7.7	6.3	15.7	4.5	2.6	3.2	17.0	8.2
2005	7.7	4.3	46.2	3.0	2.1	3.0	10.7	9.7
2006	6.4	9.1	34.6	1.9	9.6	6.6	10.6	12.9
2007	5.9	9.0	44.8	0.9	10.1	5.8	15.0	14.8

Source: UNCTAD (2008).

Remember it may cause misconception about the dynamics of FDI if we compare the "investment index" across countries without paying attention to the distinct modal distribution among them. The "investment indices" in their original formula can hardly reflect the significance of FDI for all host economies because not all FDI goes to finance new equipment and plant investments and is converted into fixed asset investment. On the global scale, an increasing proportion of FDI is to acquire existing assets of listed firms via stock markets. Cross-border mergers and acquisitions (M&As) is taking the place of greenfield investments as the dominating mode of FDI (UNCTAD, 2000). The modal distribution of FDI between M&As and greenfield investment, however, is not the same across countries. In 2007, for example, the ratio of cross-border M&As value to total FDI inflows was 89.3 percent worldwide, 30.6 percent across developing countries while only 18.6 percent in China (UNCTAD, 2008).

The varying modal distribution of FDI in different regions of the world suggests FDI inflows in developing and developed countries may have distinct implications for their host economies. Because it is usually difficult for most developing countries to launch economic growth or achieve industrial development based on productivity improvement and indigenous innovation without reaping the benefits associated with inward cross-border investment, FDI generally has a much more important effect for the industrializing economies than it does for the industrialized ones that are characterized by the existing clusters of innovation activities and strength of their advanced service sectors (Markusen, 1996; Lall, 1997 and 2000; Chang, 2002; Lall and Narula, 2004; Gereffi, Humphery et al., 2005). Thus, computing "investment indices" in its original formula may generate an upward biased estimate of the significance of FDI for developed countries.

In order to make an international comparison on the significance of FDI in its host economies, the "investment index" is adjusted in such a way that the numerator in its computation formula is equivalent in principle to investments used to purchase new equipment and plant only with those used to acquire existing assets excluded. Technically, the new numerator can be best estimated by the difference between the total FDI inflows and the value of cross-border M&A in the host economy. It then turns out that the adjusted "investment index" of China is not only well beyond that of developed countries such as the UK or the US, but also considerably greater than that of other major developing economies in the world (see Table 1.2), which is exactly opposite to the first claim based on literal interpretation of Table 1.1. What's more, if the fact that China adopts a more stringent definition of FDI (see Introduction) is taken into account, its adjusted "investment index" is supposed to be even higher than that presented in Table 1.2.

Table 1.2   The adjusted "investment indices" across countries/regions, 1990–2007 (%)

	China	US	UK	Korea	Taiwan	India	Brazil	World
1990	3.5	-0.7	-10.9	0.8	3.6	0.3	0.9	0.1
1991	3.8	-1.6	-6.3	0.5	2.9	0.1	0.6	0.8
1992	6.9	0	-2.8	0.1	0	0.3	2.9	1.0
1993	11.1	2.5	-2.6	-0.3	1.6	0.7	-0.4	1.8
1994	16.4	-0.6	-6.3	0.5	2.1	1.0	1.6	1.5
1995	14.5	0.2	-14.2	0.5	2.3	2.0	2.5	1.7
1996	13.4	0.2	-10.9	0.6	2.8	2.5	5.2	1.9
1997	13.2	-0.2	-13.3	0.8	2.4	3.3	5.6	1.7
1998	11.8	-3.5	-18.3	-0.4	0.3	2.3	3.5	0.2
1999	8.7	1.0	-25.5	-1	2.9	1.1	19.2	2.3
2000	–	-1.8	-30.1	1.6	5.5	2.1	11.3	0.7
2001	9.4	-2.5	-32.6	-0.3	2.7	4.0	17.1	1.4
2002	6.7	-2.3	-13.6	-4.5	1.4	4.2	16.8	2.1
2003	7.2	-2.2	-16.4	0.3	-0.2	2.3	8.0	2.0
2004	7.5	-1.0	-4.1	4.3	1.5	2.7	6.6	1.7
2005	6.4	-1.8	0.5	0.2	-2	1.5	8.5	0.3
2006	5.3	-0.7	-16.6	0.7	3.1	5.0	6.8	2.7
2007	4.8	-5.7	-1.4	0	2.7	4.4	11.3	1.6

Note: Not all funds that are used to finance cross-border M&As can be classified as FDI. When a domestic investor collaborates with a foreign one to acquire the shares of another domestic firm, only a portion of the MandA sale is capitalized by FDI. By subtracting the value of cross-border M&As from total FDI inflows, it may overestimate the share of cross-border M&As among total FDI inflows, which leads to the negative values in Table 1.2. This problem, however, does not change the basic pattern that China's adjusted "investment index" is much higher than that of most other countries (Graham and Wada, 2001).

Source: UNCTAD (2008).

It is also incorrect to conclude from China's declining "investment index" as shown in Table 1.2 that the share of greenfield FDI in China's total fixed asset investments, or the significance of greenfield FDI for Chinese economy, is quickly diminishing across all sectors. This book substitutes the "fixed asset investments by FIEs" for utilized FDI inflows to compute the "investment index" for individual sectors. Three reasons motivate that substitution. First of all, a portion of the FDI inflows after 2004 may be actually capitalized by international "hot money" that aims to speculate on Chinese currency appreciation or the rising real estate value (see Conclusion). That means the magnitude of FDI inflows could be an inflated parameter to estimate the significance of FDI for each individual industry in China. Secondly, "fixed asset investments by FIEs" occur within China and are directly reported in Chinese currency, which minimizes the potential risks associated with converting FDI inflows in US$ into that in Chinese currency via the constantly fluctuating exchange rate (see Appendix-1). Finally, investments used to finance cross-border M&As are already excluded from "fixed asset investments by FIEs," which makes the scope of these sector-based statistics consistent to those of the overall "investment index."

Note that only a portion of the "fixed asset investments by FIEs" is financed by FDI, and that depends on the equity share of foreign investors in the FIEs. Then the "investment index" of a sector (the columns of A×B in Table 1.3) is approximately the product of the share of "fixed asset investments by FIEs" among total fixed asset investment in that particular sector (called "investment share of FIEs" hereafter and represented by columns of A in Table 1.3) and the share of foreign capital among the registered capital of FIEs in the same sector (called "equity share of FDI" hereafter and represented by columns of B in Table 1.3). The "investment index" of real estate (column of A×B under "real estate"), for example, plummeted from 13.4 percent in 2000 to 8.4 percent in 2006, as opposed to the "investment index" of all other sectors (column of A×B under "all other sectors, excluding real estate") which increased from 4.2 percent to 6.7 percent during the same period of time or the "investment index" of manufacturing that climbed from 12.8 percent in 2000 to the summit of 15.2 percent in 2004.[2]

It is now clear that the diminishing overall "investment index" for all industries was largely caused by the booming domestic investments in the real estate sector

Table 1.3   The "investment share of FIEs" and the "equity share of FDI" of major industries, 2000–2006 (%)

	Real estate			All other sectors, excluding real estate			Manufacturing		
	A	B	A×B	A	B	A×B	A	B	A×B
2000	17.8	75.5	13.4	6.1	68.6	4.2	18.6	68.7	12.8
2001	–	–	–	–	–	–	–	–	–
2002	13.5	74.8	10.1	6.6	72.5	4.8	18.1	73.2	13.2
2003	9.8	77.5	7.6	8.6	74.4	6.4	18.3	75.2	13.8
2004	10.6	78.3	8.3	9.7	76.4	7.4	19.7	77.3	15.2
2005	10.1	79.7	8.1	9.3	77.6	7.2	18.3	78.8	14.4
2006	10.4	81.1	8.4	8.6	77.9	6.7	16.2	79	12.8

Note: 1. Columns of A and B represent the "investment share of FIEs" and the "capital share of FDI" respectively. 2. Data for 2001 is unavailable.

Source: *China Statistical Yearbook, Statistical Yearbook on Investment in Fixed Assets of China*, various years.

---

2   As shown in Table 1.3, the "investment share of FIEs" in manufacturing slightly declined in 2005 and 2006. That is most probably the outcome of the more rapidly expanding domestic investments in steel, cement, construction materials and machinery that resulted from the growth of urban real estate industry. Even under that circumstance, however, the "investment index" of manufacturing in 2006 was still as high as it was in 2000 (12.8%).

in the first decade of this century, or the fact that it would be easier for domestic investors to respond to the real estate market circumstances and make investment decisions than it was for foreign ones. Because fixed asset investment in real estate has been next only to manufacturing since 2003 (SSB, various years-a), its unusual weight among all sectors in that regard not only led to a diminishing "investment index" of real estate itself, but also generated a significant downward impact on the overall "investment index" for all industries even if the composition of domestic and foreign capital in manufacturing remains unchanged or moves in a slightly opposite direction.

1.2.2 Ascending "Size Index"

The qualitative condition of projects capitalized by FDI as measured by "size index" has been significantly improved since the early 1990s. Before 1991, a substantial share of FDI inflows were investments launched by overseas Chinese in Hong Kong, Macao and Taiwan (Wu, 1999) and the average magnitude of FDI in each project it capitalized had remained below US$1 million per project (see Figure 1.2). With increasing proportion of FDI inflows originating from developed countries, the average FDI for individual manufacturing projects reached the regional summit of US$2.76 million per project in 1996 and had been lingering between US$2 million and 3 million until 2002 when it surged again and reached the historical height of US$4.80 million in 2006. It should be noted from Figure 1.2

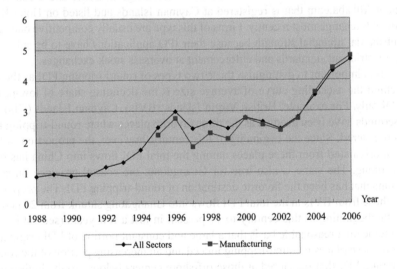

Figure 1.2   Average size of contracted FDI projects, 1988–2006 (in US$ million)

Source: *China Statistical Yearbook*, various years.

that the average size of FDI for all sectors (the solid line) is highly correlated with that in manufacturing (the dashed line).

The rising average size of FDI suggests the increasing popularity of projects with greater contracted investment on the one hand and the shrinking share of those with smaller sizes in the pool of FDI inflows on the other. Not all round-tripping FDI, however, pertains to the latter. The round-tripping FDI can be conceptually categorized into two broad types with distinct features. The first type, labeled as the *low-profile* round-tripping FDI, includes those solely motivated by the preferential policy treatments that are exclusively available to FIEs such as those mentioned in the first section of this chapter. Projects capitalized by such FDI are usually small in quantitative size and weak in qualitative strength as they do not have to possess the advantages a real foreign firm need to have. The round-tripping activities of the other type, which I would call *high-profile*, are mainly to facilitate their initial public offering (IPO) in overseas stock markets because China's domestic procedure to approve listing overseas is rather rigorous and lengthy (Zhou, 2005). As China is increasingly integrated into the world economy, more and more non-SOEs that eventually became listed in the US or Hong Kong stock markets chose to relocate themselves at offshore financial and business centers such as Hong Kong, British Virgin Islands, Bermuda and Cayman Islands. Examples include internet search engine Baidu.com which is registered at Cayman Islands and listed on Nasdaq in 2005, Home Inns that is registered at Cayman Islands and listed on Nasdaq in 2006, Qiao Xing Mobile Communication that is registered at British Virgin Islands and listed on the New York Stock Exchange in 2007, and e-commerce giant Alibaba.com that is registered at Cayman Islands and listed on Hong Kong Stock Exchange most recently. Firms of this type are usually competitive ones with substantial financial strength because their IPO applications have to be subject to more stringent standards and enforcement at overseas stock exchanges.

It is important to distinguish these two types of round-tripping FDI as the fact behind the ascending curve of average size is the declining share of low-profile FDI only. For example, British Virgin Islands (BVIs), Cayman Islands (CIs) and Bermuda have been deemed as the three favorite places where round-tripping FDI is registered. Since the beginning of this century, however, the proportion of FDI that originated from these places among the total FDI flows into China has been declining. The same is also true for Guangdong, the coastal province on south China that has been the favorite destination of round-tripping FDI. The proportion of those from BVIs in the total FDI flows into Guangdong shrank from 21 percent at the beginning of this century to 17 percent in just a few years (see Table 1.4). Assume on a reasonable basis that a large and constant portion of FDI originating from these places is round-tripping indeed and an increasing portion of the round-tripping FDI that registered at those off-shore centers belongs to the high-profile type. Then the information presented in Table 1.4 suggests a sharply declining share of low-profile round-tripping FDI as well as a constant or rising share of high-profile type among all FDI inflows in China in recent few years.

Table 1.4   Shares of contracted FDI originating from three offshore centers in the total contracted FDI inflows, 2000–2006 (%)

	FDI in China (=100%)			FDI in Guangdong (=100%)		
	BVIs	CIs	Bermuda	BVIs	CIs	Bermuda
2000	12.05	5.03	0.89	20.9	2.4	0.1
2001	12.68	2.33	0.37	21.5	1.2	0.0
2002	15.28	2.73	0.87	20.0	1.2	0.3
2003	11.00	1.47	0.26	17.5	2.6	0.5
2004	12.64	2.11	0.50	18.7	2.0	1.6
2005	11.65	1.80	0.32	18.1	1.8	0.9
2006	–	–	–	17.1	1.7	0.5

Note: The contracted rather than utilized FDI inflows are used because the purpose here is to observe the extent to which round-tripping FDI can get eventually accepted in China but not its actual impacts on the host economy.

Source: China Foreign Economic Statistical Yearbook, 2006, Almanac of China's Foreign Economic Relations and Trade, Guangdong Statistical Yearbook, various years.

The above analysis about the dynamics of round-tripping FDI draws upon indirect deduction instead of direct statistics that are rarely available in a consistent and reliable way. Most quantitative analysis on round-tripping FDI is based on data extrapolation either from China's balance of payments or contrasting statistics from different countries (World Bank, 2002a; Xiao, 2004). Perhaps a stronger piece of empirical evidence for the improved quality of FDI projects as suggested by the rising "size index" is the dynamics of Other Foreign Investments (OFI). Remember it requires a minimum of 25 percent share of stakes in the direct investment enterprise in order to be defined as FDI in China. When the share of foreign invested capital in an enterprise falls below that threshold, it is categorized by Chinese statistics as OFI in which Processing and Assembly (PA) is the dominating type. Specifically, PA means the foreign party typically supplies machinery, designs, components or raw materials and the Chinese party assembles or processes these according to quality requirements as specified by the foreign partner who receives the finished products. The Chinese party will be paid a processing fee in return for which the installment price of the machinery and so on may be deducted.

Just like low-profile round-tripping FDI, foreign investments in PA are generally characterized by small sizes as well as low content of technology. As a popular form of business cooperation between Hong Kong and mainland Chinese firms, PA is also found to be quite popular in the province of Guangdong because of its geographical proximity to Hong Kong as well as low costs associated with moving the supplies and products back and forth. As illustrated in Table 1.5, the share of foreign capital invested in PA among total foreign investments (the sum of FDI and OFI) has generally been decreasing from the start of this century in both China and Guangdong. That lends further support to the notion that projects capitalized by small-size foreign investment, whether it is low-profile FDI or PA, are losing the market shares they used to have in mainland China, while those with considerable magnitudes of investments and advanced technology and management are gaining increasing popularity.

Table 1.5   Shares of foreign capital contracted in PA among the total foreign investments, 1999–2006 (%)

	PA/ (FDI+OFI)	
	China	Guangdong
1999	4.0	20.0
2000	2.5	15.9
2001	2.5	11.1
2002	2.2	9.2
2003	1.4	6.6
2004	1.7	11.2
2005	1.8	–
2006	1.6	10.6

Source: *China Statistical Yearbook, Guangdong Statistical Yearbook*, various years.

1.3 Toward a Demand-Side Perspective

To a large extent, the dynamics of "investment index" and "size index" is correlated to that of contracted FDI inflows over the four periods as demonstrated before. For example, China's "investment index" had been less than 3 percent in the 1980s (UNCTAD, 2008) and the "size index" was still below US$1 million at the end of the 1980s (see Figure 1.2). When the magnitude of contracted FDI inflows soared in the early 1990s, both indices were upsurging as well. After that, "investment index" for greenfield FDI in Chinese manufacturing industries has been maintained on an level unparalleled by most other countries in the world and the "size index" rose again from the start of this century.

Such a pattern highlights two critical periods during which FDI was most vibrant in China. One is the early 1990s which was characterized by the influx of FDI as well as by a quickly rising "investment index" and "size index." Although the opening of Pudong in 1990 and Deng's southern tour in 1992 may play a role in boosting the FDI inflows, that can hardly explain why Chinese domestic investments did not gain a proportional growth. The other is the first decade of this century with surging FDI inflows, rocketing "size index" and "investment index" for greenfield manufacturing FDI that has been unattainable for most other countries, which, as mentioned before, may not be solely attributed to the recovery of world economy following Asian financial crisis. In order to understand the causes underlying the pattern of FDI in China, this section starts with a brief review of those theories most relevant to FDI and concludes with the implication for a perspective that incorporates China's domestic demand for manufacturing FDI into this book's analysis.

1.3.1 How does FDI Arise: Advantages and Internalization

It is Hymer (1976) who initially argued that foreign firms must possess some firm-specific advantages over their domestic rivals in order to succeed overseas because investing abroad, as mentioned before, usually incurs greater costs associated with cultural, linguistic as well as legal and political adaptation. These ownership-specific advantages (O-advantages) were specifically identified by Kindleberger (1969) as brand names, management and marketing skills, proprietary technology, financial strength, economies of scale and so on. How the advantages of FDI in one or some of these aspects affect its performance overseas has been addressed by many scholars. For example, Caves (1974 and 2007) emphasized possession of intangible assets by MNCs allowed them to differentiate products in the market and secure stream of cash flows. In the approach of "new economic geography", economist Krugman (1991) showed how a firm's advantage in scale led to specialized production and the ensuing trade activities. Although Krugman did not explicitly address FDI, it is transaction cost, or "iceberg cost" in his core-periphery model, that motivates the internalization strategy and gives rise to FDI.

   The basic notion of transaction costs was originally articulated by Coase (1937) to address the organization issue of a firm. According to him, it was to deter the frictions associated with external market that a firm was organized through the hierarchical control inside its own boundary. In line with this reasoning, Chandler (1977) argued for the advantages of "visible hand" over contractual transactions in organizing production and management. To the extent that his largely descriptive achievement lacked an underlying theory of organizational change, it is Williamson (1981) who linked the Chandlerian firm to the theory of transaction costs as founded by the ground-breaking works of Coase. In Williamson's account, the vertical integrated firm, as the product of a series of organizational innovations that have had the purpose and effect of economizing on transaction costs, arose because asset specificity and asymmetric information usually disinclined independent market partners from investing in necessary assets and exerting adequate efforts (Williamson, 1981). In light of all sorts of costs and uncertainties associated with market transactions, the advantage built upon the strategy of internalization (I-advantages) is another weapon of firms in addition to the scale in Krugman's model, which prompted the argument that the failure of international intermediate product markets at that time is both a necessary and sufficient condition to explain the existence of MNCs (Buckley and Casson 1985).

The efforts of internalization, however, are being seriously challenged by the rise of alliance capitalism (Piore and Sabel, 1984). A rapidly growing literature on industrial districts suggests that the leviathan enterprise is under siege from panoply of disintegrated firms that can respond to highly differentiated market demand in a flexible way. The rise of those disintegrated firms, however, is a complement to, instead of substitute for, MNCs that still exercise power and influence over production (Gereffi and Bonacich, 1994). In reality, MNCs retain *de facto* command over production not only by shifting toward such core functions as strategic design, final assembly, distribution and marketing that incorporate their ownership advantage in technological research and development, but also through maintaining direct control over manufacturing activities – especially in industries characterized by proprietary technologies, brand names and other intangible assets – that are being relocated overseas. Williamson (1975), for example, also examined the deficiencies associated with both markets and hierarchies. When the internal organization is more efficient than the market, the failure of the market occurs, and *vice versa*. This is the relative efficiency between these two modes that determines which is to be adopted for each particular transaction.

Firms with ownership of know-how then actively seek spatial expansion either to preserve their proprietary advantages or to collect localized information from the destination markets. One of the reasons for the effectiveness of internalization in the face of quickly diminishing transportation and communication costs is the "public" nature of those knowledge-based products. If production characterized by technological know-how can be imitated by peer firms with ease, it will substantially cut the private return to the original owner. As Lall (2000) put it, the growing reluctance of MNCs (the technological leaders) to part with valuable technologies to unrelated firms meant greater reliance on FDI to obtain new technologies. Thus many spin-offs from conventional vertically integrated firms, according to Vernon (1966), are just featured with technology that usually lags behind its current world frontier. Besides, in order to gain insights into the preference of customers in the destination market, it is important to maintain closer spatial proximity to them by setting up physical establishment there.

1.3.2 Where does FDI Go: Location-Specific Factors

Although the ownership-specific advantages or the internalization strategy may explain the existence of FDI as opposed to contractual alliance, most of these arguments fail to account for the issue of location where FDI eventually takes place. The only exception is "new economic geography" according to which whether or not FDI will take place depends on the balance between the "iceberg cost" on one hand and costs associated with establishing equipment and plant abroad on the other. The implication is the location-specific features are critical to the occurrence of FDI in that particular place.

The earliest systematic efforts to incorporate location factors into the analytical framework of FDI should be attributed to British scholar John Dunning (1980 and 1995) who proposed the eclectic paradigm to address international production issues. According to Dunning, FDI takes place where firms can combine their ownership-specific advantages with the location-specific advantages of host countries via internalization to maximize profits. Conventionally, these location-specific advantages include cultural proximity, cheap labor and rapid economic growth of host countries. Culture, as usually perceived in location-related studies, involves linguistic familiarity, customary homogeneity and kinship ties. Other things being equal, it is natural that cross-border direct investment happens where it can find such proximity. That can be interpreted either via the easiness to accumulate social capital or the aversion to transaction costs triggered by cultural incompatibility. The problem with this perspective, however, lies in its deficiency in explaining the volatile FDI dynamics, as culture does not change over a short period of time. It is then difficult to understand the vicissitude of FDI inflows of China as driven by cultural adaptability.

If the cultural account no longer has the effectiveness which it used to have at the beginning of China's opening, the economic variables such as cheap labor, excellent infrastructure or high growth rate are frequently cited as factors sparking the enthusiasm of foreign investors. However, arguments based on low cost of labor or logistics may no longer be tenable in the face of international comparison because many other countries which have either cheaper labor or more developed infrastructure receive far fewer FDI inflows than China does. Although high growth rate of the host economy sounds convincing for the sake of the positive correlation between it and FDI inflows, it is subject to the problem of endogeneity because the causal direction between FDI and growth of the host economy may exist in both ways. For example, FIEs generated nearly 30 percent of the national total industrial output, 60 percent of the export, and 20 percent of the fixed asset investment in manufacturing (see Table I.1 and 1.3). For a country whose economic growth is largely driven by fixed asset investments and export, such extraordinary performance means a significant portion of China's GDP growth was contributed by FIEs.

The above perspectives as well as most existing studies on the location choice of FDI are unanimously concerned with the location-specific advantages to which FDI is sensitive. They are either country-specific factors including market size, preferential policies, labor costs or a hybrid of all (Chen, Chang et al., 1995; Wei, 1995; Naughton, 1996; Liu, Song et al., 1997; Jiang, Christodoulou et al., 2001; He, 2005), or sub-national region-based features such as agglomeration economy (Head and Ries, 1996; Qu and Green, 1997; Cheng and Kwan, 2000; Sun, Tong et al., 2002), infrastructure provision (Chen 1996; Broadman and Sun, 1997; Hou and Zhang, 2001) or the formal institutions that make investment abroad less costly than they are supposed to be (Gong, 1995; Luo, 1997; Fu, 2000). The exclusive focus of these accounts on the external factors that motivate FDI, however, makes them unable to supply a satisfactory account for the high "investment index" of China that this book is going to investigate because domestic investments may in principle benefit from the culture homogeneity, cheap labor, excellent infrastructure and rapid economic growth as well as FDI does. In other words, only those location-specific factors that appeal to FDI on one hand and are unavailable to domestic investors on the other could be held responsible for its pervasive presence in China.

One example of such location-specific advantage is the institutions specially devised for FDI. Conceptually, there are two broad types of institutions. One is based on the impersonal rational authority that includes legal regulations and official policies. The main function of such institutions is to reduce the friction associated with transaction processes and promote efficiency and prosperity (North, 1990). As cross-border direct investment is usually a complex process that involves a series of transactions across considerable temporal range and geographical distance, most of those formal institutions on regulating the daily operations of FIEs are designed to minimize the unfamiliarity they may have with the business practice of the host country and do not constitute an exclusive advantage for FDI over domestic investment. Although some other formal institutions such as legitimate tax concession to FIEs do provide foreign direct investors certain privileges,[3] they can hardly account for the high "investment index" or rising "size index" in China. The reason is that the differential tax treatments of China are mainly designed to offset the inherent biases in planned economy that naturally favor the SOEs rather than constitute a special advantage of FIEs (Huang, 2003). Besides, special tax incentives have been widely used as a measure to attract FDI in many countries in the world (Fletcher, 2002), but few have an "investment index" as high as, or even close to, that of China. A survey of foreign investors in OECD countries, for example, found that the tax incentive was one of the least important parameters that determine the prospect of success overseas and influence the decision of whether or not to invest (OECD, 1995).

The other type of institution refers to the informal norms of behaviors or conventions of mind underlying the territorial landscape of economic development. One example of such a "soft institution" with regard to FDI is the hospitality of Chinese local governments toward cross-border investors. Quite a few analyzed the interaction between them at the city of Kunshan where a great deal of manufacturing FDI agglomerates (Yang, 1998; Po, 2003). The municipal government made every effort to build a highly competitive environment where projects capitalized by FDI can operate efficiently. Some path-breaking initiatives were even against the rigid socialist state-approval system. They even proactively involved investors in the daily decision-making processes to form a cross-border coalition consisting of both cross-border capitalists and local representatives. Such treatment, however, is extremely rare with domestic investors who have been

---

3   The Law of PRC on EIT that unified the EIT rate of both FIEs and domestic firms into the uniform rate of 25 percent also granted FIEs a five-year grace period during which their EIT rate was gradually raised from 18 percent in 2008, 20 percent in 2009, 22 percent in 2010 and 24 percent in 2011 to 25 percent in 2012 (State Council, 2007). That means FIEs are still eligible for a lower EIT rate than domestic firms before 2012.

plagued by the lack of financial and legal support in an asymmetrical manner (Huang, 2003). Such contrasting treatments conferring enormous advantages on FIEs over their domestic rivals not only clearly mirror the hunger of Chinese local governments for FDI inflows, but also shift our focus from supply-side factors that interest FDI to demand-side causes that prioritize it.

Chapter 2
Rise of Entrepreneurial Local States

The hunger for manufacturing FDI is a vivid representation of the entrepreneurial orientation of Chinese local states to achieve short-term economic and revenue growth. The term "local" in studies of China's politics refers to provincial, municipal, county or intra-urban district scales that are all under the central state in a hierarchical system (Chung, 1999; White, 1991). Although the overarching institutional structure as will be illustrated in this chapter mobilizes local state entrepreneurialism on all levels, municipal governments have the most substantial space and substantive power to spur such growth. In contrast, provincial governments are subject to immediate supervision of the center and are largely devoid of direct control over tangible assets such as urban land that can be used to build the entrepreneurial project (Fitzgerald, 2002; Hendrischke and Feng, 1999). On the other hand, the jurisdiction duties of county-level or district-level governments are stipulated by the municipal government and they do not have great administrative or financial latitudes as a result (Zhang and Wu, 2006).

By examining China's centralized political system as well as its shifting fiscal schemes, this chapter will investigate its immediate impact on the local demand for manufacturing FDI in the early 1990s. More importantly, analysis of this political economic structure will demonstrate how it gives rise to the dominating weight of manufacturing and real estate in the Chinese economy. Local state used in this chapter conceptually involves different levels of governments as specified above that are all subject to the political and fiscal regimes, though to slightly varying degrees with the latter. As specific land-based tactics will be addressed to demonstrate how the growth of these two sectors eventually leads to the FDI pattern as identified in Chapter 1, which is demand-side preference for manufacturing FDI over domestic investment and projects capitalized by greater investment over otherwise, local state will be specifically confined to the municipal sphere as a particular illustration of its entrepreneurialism on that level.

2.1 Features of Local State Entrepreneurialism

A rapidly growing literature has been developed since the end of 1980s to explore the rise of state entrepreneurialism across the world (Harvey, 1989; Hall and Hubbard, 1996; Young and Kaczmarek, 1999; Jessop and Sum, 2000). Although local states have generally been viewed as entrepreneurial market builders when they proactively orchestrate the different market actors into a project of structural competitiveness building, we have to remain cautious when the term "entrepreneurial" is used for local states in the context of China because it involves intrinsic features that distinguish Chinese local states from those in the Schumpeterian sense and the conventional developmental state.

Originally a concept to describe the motivation behind "creative destruction," the Schumpeterian entrepreneurialism is usually used as the equivalent of technological and organizational innovation that drives the capitalist development. In order to promote local economic development that is based on the clustering of creative talents (Florida, 2002 and 2005) or competitive firms (Porter, 1998), local states must posit themselves as *market builders* by creating environmental amenities and support institutions to attract such mobile productive factors. On the other hand, the concept of developmental state that is quite appealing to the Chinese government comes from Japanese and Korean experience in fostering key industrial sectors to catch up with the industrialized West (Woo-Cumings, 1999). By breaking the monopolizing ideology of liberalism dominating the US and UK in the 1980s, success of this "state governing the market" strategy shows the validity of state as a *market regulator* engaging itself in strategic management in late industrializing countries.

The role played by Chinese local states, however, is moving away from the market builder in the Schumpeterian sense or the market regulator of the developmental state toward a *market actor* that aims to achieve tangible urban economic and physical growth on a short-term basis. For example, municipalities heavily depend on manufacturing and real estate as the major engines of economic

Table 2.1   Sectoral distribution of national business tax, VAT and EIT revenues, 2002–2006 (%)

		2002	2003	2004	2005	2006
Business Tax (=100%)	Real estate	16.8	21.5	22.8	23.5	25.0
	Construction	20.9	23.3	22.8	23.3	23.1
	Finance	17.7	14.2	13.2	13.1	13.7
VAT (=100%)	Manufacturing	58.9	60.8	59.2	58.5	57.9
	W & R trade	17.7	17.4	12.4	17.3	17.2
	Public utilities	11.7	11.7	8.2	11.0	11.1
EIT (=100%)	Manufacturing	26.4	26.4	26.5	24.1	19.5
	W & R trade	–	16.7	17.6	15.9	14.3
	Mining	12.8	11.1	14.5	15.3	15.1

Note: 1. The percentages presented here are based on national figures, which do not affect our assessment about the sectoral distribution of local budgetary revenues. The reason is that VAT and EIT are shared between the central and local governments according to fixed rates and business tax is entirely retained at the local level. 2. "W & R" denotes wholesale and retail.

Source: *Tax Yearbook of China*, various years.

growth and major sources of fiscal revenues, while sectors of advanced services and creative production whose growth requires multi-year efforts on institutional or cultural building have remained admittedly weak even after almost 30 years since 1978. Table 2.1 presented the percentage contributions of major sectors to the national revenues of business tax, value-added tax (VAT) and EIT that are the largest three sources of local tax revenues. For business tax, the proportions of real estate and construction have been constantly rising from 2002 to 2006 while that of finance steadily declined during the same period. Manufacturing is the largest contributor to both VAT and EIT with more than half of VAT and one fourth of EIT generated by this broad sector. Given the weight of business tax, VAT and EIT in local budgetary revenues, these demonstrate the critical significance of investments in manufacturing and real estate for the financial strength of Chinese local governments.

A stronger piece of evidence for the critical significance of manufacturing and real estate is the complete sectoral distribution of local tax revenues. Unlike the approach used in Table 2.1, however, it is incorrect here to estimate the local tax revenue collected from each sector by multiplying the corresponding national figure by a uniform rate of sharing because the tax contributions by each sector are collected from a range of tax categories that are subject to different schemes of sharing between the central and local government. It is necessary to disaggregate the national tax revenue of each sector on the basis of individual tax category, the sharing rate of which is approximately the ratio of local to national revenues collected under that particular item. For example, the national tax contribution by manufacturing comes from VAT, EIT and other tax categories. The ratio of local to national VAT can be deemed as the local sharing rate for VAT. Summing up the products of the national tax revenues and the sharing rates across all tax categories would be the local tax revenues contributed by each sector. As shown in Table 2.2, tax revenues associated with manufacturing are much greater than those of any other listed sectors. The second and third largest contributors to local tax revenues

Table 2.2   Sectoral distribution of local tax revenues, 2002–2006 (in billion yuan)

	2002	2003	2004	2005	2006
Manufacturing	167.94	187.19	282.87	272.97	267.68
Real Estate	51.52	76.79	107.10	136.62	181.15
Construction	57.87	75.42	93.14	112.99	135.70
W & R Trade	–	67.66	84.70	99.89	93.46
Finance	55.58	54.51	62.24	82.46	113.28
Mining	32.36	32.78	48.03	70.06	69.77
Public Utilities	28.00	30.17	34.68	39.74	48.59

Source: *Tax Yearbook of China*, various years.

are real estate and construction respectively. During the four years from 2002 to 2006, local tax revenues collected from these two sectors almost tripled, a rate of growth that is unparalleled even by manufacturing.

In addition to the financial dependence on manufacturing and real estate for revenues, Chinese local states are also characterized by their expenditures deviating from fields closely related to civic life such as education, medical care and social security. Table 2.3 lists the ratios of local final to budgetary expenditures for the largest seven expenditure items between 2000 and 2006. Values greater than 1 means the final actual expenditure exceeds the projected level, and *vice versa*. Although it is entirely natural that the final actual expenditures by the end of each year may not exactly conform to the budgetary figures projected at the beginning of that year, deviation on a systematic basis as measured by the ratios between these two figures may also shed light on the spending preference of local governments. In most years during this period, the ratios of final to projected expenditures for capital construction (item 1), urban maintenance and construction (item 4) as well as government administration (items 7), all exceeded the average, which reflects the expanding size of Chinese local governments and their extensive expenditures on physical projects.

It is widely reported on numerous Chinese domestic mass media that the construction of mega-projects such as city halls, public squares, exhibition centers as well as state-of-art stadiums is a increasingly contagious phenomenon across many Chinese cities (CCTV, 2007a and 2007b), to which even some hinterland

Table 2.3   Ratios of the actual to projected expenditures, 2001–2006

	2001	2002	2003	2004	2005	2006
1. Capital construction	1.60	1.13	1.08	1.05	1.16	0.94
2. Innovation funds & science and technology funds	1.08	0.88	1.08	1.09	1.10	1.09
3. Supporting agricultural production	1.09	1.10	0.94	1.43	0.92	1.08
4. Urban maintenance and construction	1.08	1.10	1.11	1.16	1.20	1.06
5. Culture, education, science & health care	1.10	1.06	1.04	1.05	1.04	1.09
6. Social security	1.26	1.16	0.96	0.99	0.96	0.95
7. Government administration	1.16	1.11	1.10	1.11	1.09	1.06
All items	1.14	1.04	1.04	1.08	1.06	1.06

Source: *Finance Yearbook of China*, various years.

distressed towns are no exceptions (Xiao and Wang, 2007). The irrational overspending on public projects regardless of social benefits and capital costs (Jin and Zou, 2003) suggests the metaphor of corporate firms (Duckett, 1998; Oi, 1992 and 1996; Walder, 1995) may not be an accurate portrait of today's Chinese entrepreneurial local state because the cost side of government initiatives is not taken into their balanced considerations. As Wu (2007) commented, when strategic promotion and public investments initiated by the local states are undertaken without significant pressure to take genuine demand and balancing financial capacity into consideration, the "entrepreneurial" orientations of Chinese local states may exist in form but not in essence.

In contrast, the local expenditure on social items such as agricultural production (item 3) or culture, education, science and health care (item 5) either lacks a consistent pattern over time or does not gain the rate of growth that is proportional to the overall average. More illustratively, the actual expenditure on social security (item 6) by Chinese local states had been less than the originally projected levels for four consecutive years since 2003. Such a pattern of fiscal spending is also echoed by the studies of Li (2008) and Chen (2008a and 2008b) which show Chinese governmental spending on items of health care, social security and unemployment insurance was merely 461 *yuan* per capita (equivalent to 3 percent of average individual disposable income) or 2.4 percent of its GDP, while it was 5,000 US$ (equivalent to 18 percent of average individual disposable income) or 11.5 percent of its GDP for the US even though the fiscal strengths of these two countries as measured relative to their own GDP are quite close to each other (20 percent of its GDP for China and 18 percent of its GDP for the US). These manifest the manipulated distribution of public resources by the local states away from social public services, which eventually left increasing number of the urban poor less protected from the state-led process of economic restructuring and urban growth (Chen, Gu et al., 2006; Liu and Wu, 2006).

2.2 Political Economic Foundations of Local State Entrepreneurialism

The rise of the local state entrepreneurialism as profiled above is the outcome of the political economic structure of China. On one hand, the centralized personnel evaluation and selection system strongly motivates local officials on the lower levels to maximize the urban economic and physical growth within their office terms. That in turn fuels the growth of manufacturing and real estate and motivates the extravagant local public spending on capital and construction projects. On the other, the recentralized fiscal scheme institutionalized in 1994 forced local states to raise their budgetary revenues to match the heavier expenditure responsibilities, which, however, can hardly be accomplished without substantial manufacturing FDI inflows.

2.2.1 Centralized Political System

The rapid economic growth of Chinese economy has been conventionally attributed to the decentralized fiscal and administrative structure of China (Qian and Xu, 1993; Qian and Weingast, 1996; Lin and Liu, 2000). However, either the recentralized fiscal system since 1994 (Jin and Zou, 2005) or the more recent efforts of Beijing to recentralize regulations on environmental protection, food safety and land use (Zhou, 2007) are not incompatible with the outstanding economic performance of China. That suggests a more fundamental driver of China's economic growth underlying the reforms in its fiscal and administrative fields. In contrast to the progress China has made in the realm of economic reform, its political institutions that are characterized by a centralized system of personnel control, with most local officials appointed from above, has remained largely intact even to this day (World Bank, 2002b).[1] The preservation of the overall political institutions does not mean that there has been no change at all to the criteria according to which officials get appointed or promoted. While "economic development" took the place of "class struggle" as the dominating national ideology, a crucial turnaround in personnel management has involved the wholesale shift in the evaluation criteria for government officials from political conformity to the economic performance achieved within their jurisdictions.

The centralized political system in which the appointment of officials is largely based on the economic performance achieved under their leadership plays a critical role in the economic growth of China (Blanchard and Shleifer, 2000). As we now understand, "economic development" consists of the quantitative and qualitative aspects of economic dynamics. The asymmetric information between different levels of governments, however, makes it extremely costly, if not impossible, for officials on a higher level to learn the qualitative conditions of local economies such as environmental sustainability, economic equality and social justice. The more readily available information on the local economic performance is on its quantitative magnitude as either measured by indicators of local GDP, fiscal revenues and FDI inflows or sensed from the concrete projects like modern infrastructure, mega-projects of art and sports and high-rise buildings. Although successful accomplishment of social targets such as implementing birth control, maintaining social stability and raising school enrolments are also the criteria to determine performance (Edin, 2003), most of them are merely "pass" or "fail" indicators and do not create full incentives for officials to compete against one another. Thus the real grading system in which officials can be ranked for political promotion is still based on the tangible economic and/or physical achievements. Thus, a rapidly growing local economy represented by sanguine

---

1   As rural villages and urban communities are defined as community organizations rather than a level of state administration, the grass-roots leadership elections that have been taking place quite extensively across these territories do not qualify as selections to state governmental offices. See Tao, Lin et al. (2004) and Xu (2004).

economic indicators and grand physical projects becomes an important political incentive or career concern on the part of Chinese local officials who unanimously engage themselves in the yardstick competition for economic performance within their own jurisdictions as well as for the associated personal political promotion (Li and Zhou, 2005). Regular bureaucrats also benefit from such growth because a considerable proportion of their incomes are institutionally related to the economic strength of the region or sector they are affiliated with (Zhu, 2008).

In addition, the office term of political appointment forces officials to materialize the achievements within that duration of a few years. The evaluation system based on short-term economic performance discourages major initiatives to build competitive sectors of advanced services that usually require a wide range of support institutions such as intellectual property rights protection, venture capital market, creative milieu, or even the openness and competitiveness of a country's political system (North, 2005). The establishment of all these is well beyond simple government fiats and can hardly be accomplished within a few years. In contrast, attracting inward investments in manufacturing and real estate is a much easier approach to boost local economy and improve urban physical conditions than improving technological or organizational efficiency that would be impossible without continuing efforts over a much longer period. This is not to disclaim the increasing significance of advanced service sectors or technology-intensive industries for Chinese growth. Rather, it means that manufacturing and real estate remain the critical drivers of Chinese urban economic growth, to which even cities positing themselves as China's high-tech and financial centers are not exceptions. For example, one half of Shanghai's GDP in 2007 came from manufacturing and real estate (Shanghai Municipal Statistical Bureau, 2008). In 2006, nearly 54 percent of the total fixed asset investments in Beijing occurred in the sector of real estate that generated 15 percent of the municipal tax revenues in 2008 (SSB, various years; Ren, 2009).

Besides, as will be elaborated in the next chapter, the prosperity of real estate markets can also brings the local governments a great deal of "land granting premium" which is the critical financial resource to enable the large-scale urban construction. The consequence, as Kenneth Lieberthal (1995 and 1997) observed, is that Chinese local states now simply focus on short-term revenue-maximizing and image-building. Work related to structural adjustment and long-term development that is crucial to the national competitiveness is just not within the scope of their concerns.

2.2.2 Fiscal Decentralization and Recentralization

In the context of a centralized political system where the political prospects of local officials largely depend on the economic performance achieved under their leadership, both the decentralized fiscal system before and the recentralized fiscal scheme after 1994 act as the driver of the rapid economic growth of China. Fiscal decentralization and recentralization are defined here through changing relative fiscal strength of the central and local governments. For example, fiscal decentralization is represented by the declining share of central government in national tax revenues before 1994 (see Table 2.5) while recentralization after 1994 is characterized by the reverse (see Table 2.8).

On the basis of a schematic description of their main features, this section will highlight how the effect of "whip the fast and hard-working ox" (*bian da kuai niu*) associated with all decentralized fiscal systems led to the extensive presence of local SOEs before 1994, and how the recentralized scheme institutionalized that year motivated the growth of manufacturing and real estate sectors, which is prerequisite to understand the patter of FDI since the beginning of this century. It will also show FDI influx in the early 1990s as a result of expecting the switch between these two systems.

2.2.2.1 Decentralized fiscal systems before 1994

In many years before 1980 when China decided to open its doors to the outside world, it had maintained a highly planned economic system. China's fiscal system was characterized by centralized revenue collection and centralized expenditure disbursing. Only rather limited revenue-sharing schemes between central and provincial governments existed between 1949 and 1980 (Lardy, 1975). Very few surpluses could be retained on the provincial or lower level. Local governments acted simply like an executive agent of the center and do not have their own independent interests (Wong, 1995; Riskin, 2000). It was realized that in order to promote economic growth greater flexibility should be decentralized to localities by letting the sub-national governments retain greater powers in financing their own needs. Since 1980, the highly centralized fiscal system had gone through a series of reform initiatives to establish the "fiscal responsibility system," that is, to specify the particular revenue sources and broad expenditure responsibilities for the central and local governments respectively. Although most of the fiscal schemes were originally designed only for the relationship between the central and provincial governments, arrangements were also contracted between the latter and local governments under their administration in a similar fashion.

The fiscal scheme of 1980 laid out the basic configurations of subsequent reforms. Based on the one implemented in Sichuan province in 1979 (named "Sichuan Model" hereafter), this scheme divided all revenues in 15 provinces into four categories: central fixed revenue, local fixed revenue, shared revenue at fixed ratio and adjustable revenue (see Table 2.4).[2] Provinces whose total revenues

---

2   There are a few regional exceptions to this contract responsibility system that had the broadest geographical coverage. Firstly, in Jiangsu province as well as the three centrally administered municipalities of Beijing, Tianjin and Shanghai, all fiscal revenues, instead of being divided into the four categories, were pooled together then shared with the center according to an overall rate that was determined on the basis of their respective revenues and expenditures of past few years. The reason that the "Sichuan Model" was not extended to these regions/cities was that their remittances constituted a considerable share

including local fixed revenues and their part of shared revenues exceeded their total expenditures had to remit a portion of their balances to the center. If the total revenues could not meet expenditures, provinces were then eligible for a portion of the adjustable revenues. When the adjustable revenues were still inadequate to make up the deficits, the provinces would be subsidized by a fixed amount transfer payment. Budget revenues and expenditures in 1979 were used as the "base figures" to determine the rate of local-to-central remittance, the proportion of adjustable revenues that could be retained by the localities and the amount of central-to-local subsidies, so as to meet the expenditure needs of individual localities with their budgetary revenues. Once determined, these rates and amounts were fixed for a five-year period and would be renewed only at the end of the fifth year according to the revenues and expenditures during the past five years. That is to say, given a certain level of expenditure, the less local revenue collected in the past five years, the lower the rate of local-to-central remittance, the higher the proportion of adjustable revenue that could be locally retained or the amount of central-to-local subsidies for the next five years. Similarly, localities with given revenues would also receive these benefits in the next five years if they had higher current expenditure figures.

Table 2.4   The revenue sharing scheme of 1980

	Sources
Central fixed revenues	1. Profits from centrally owned enterprises 2. Customs duty 3. Industrial and commercial tax from rail
Local fixed revenues	1. Profits from locally owned enterprises 2. Salt tax 3. Agricultural tax 4. Business income tax
Shared revenue at fixed ratio	Profits of enterprises whose ownership were transferred from localities to the center were shared at a rate of 80 to 20 between the central and local governments
Adjustable revenues	Industrial and commercial tax

Source: Agarwala (1992), p. 66.

of central treasure coffer. Before the effects of the "Sichuan Model" became visible, the center needed to secure its revenues sources from these places. See Song (1992), p. 50, for details. Secondly, for the eight provinces or minority autonomous regions in western China including Inner Mongolia, Xinjiang, Tibet, Ningxia, Guangxi, Yunnan, Qinghai, Guizhou, they were allowed to retain all incremental revenues beyond their respective "base figures" and the subsidies they received from the central government would increase at an annual rate of 10 percent. Finally, for the coastal provinces of Guangdong and Fujian where the first four SEZs were established, they were given wider fiscal latitude by remitting or receiving a lump-sum amount to or from the center.

Since benefits which the localities could expect in the future were institutionalized to be negatively related to their current revenues, it greatly discouraged local efforts to mobilize the collection of budgetary revenues, an effect called "whip the fast and hard-working ox" (Ahmad, Li et al., 2002), which in turn led to the rapid growth of "extra-budgetary" funds on one hand and declining ratios of budgetary revenue to GDP on the other. In China, all fiscal schemes are built on the basis of revenues officially collected and channeled to the Ministry of Finance at Beijing, which is usually called *"yu suan nei"* or "budgetary" system. The other source of governmental revenues is what is known as *"yu suan wai"* or "extra-budgetary" funds that usually consist of a variety of non-tax fees and they remain entirely at the local levels without having to be reported in the regular budgetary accounts. As the profits remitted by SOEs were designated as budgetary revenue, local governments were then motivated to conceal their budgetary revenues by imposing ad hoc fees on those enterprises within their jurisdictions, a practice widely known as *"tan pai"* or "mandatory assignments," so that a portion of the profits that were supposed to be counted as local budgetary revenues was transformed into the extra-budgetary funds.

The "tax-for-profit" reform in 1983 that substituted the EIT levied on the profits of SOEs for the complete profits remittance by them did not affect the local strategy of "concealing revenues."[3] Because post-tax profits could be dispensed by enterprises independently and they no longer belonged to local budgetary revenues, local governments usually granted illicit tax concessions to enterprises they owned in order to acquire a significantly lower figure of budgetary revenues while compensating their loss in the tax revenues by charging those enterprises ad hoc fees. More often than not, the benefits of tax concession were completely counteracted by the costs of these charges, which made the enterprises worse off (see section 2.2.3 in this chapter). As a result, the magnitude of local extra-budgetary funds more than doubled from 53.2 billion *yuan* in 1982 all the way to 120.08 billion in 1987 (see the second column of Table 2.5) even though China's central government took stringent measures to control their growth and use.[4] On the other hand, the growth of budgetary revenues lagged increasingly behind that of the national economy. The ratio of national budgetary revenues to GDP,

---

3   See footnote 1 in Chapter 1 for details of the "tax-for-profit" reform.

4   To curb the growth of the local extra-budgetary funds, the central government forcibly borrowed 8 billion, 7 billion and 4 billion *yuan* respectively from provinces in three consecutive years of 1980, 1981 and 1982. Effective from 1 January 1983, 10 percent of all extra-budgetary revenue was collected by the central government as the "state fund in energy and communication key construction." That rate was raised to 15 percent in the second half of 1983. On the use of extra-budgetary funds, local governments were required to turn a full accounting of them in to the Ministry of Finance. In addition, a construction tax of 10 percent was to be assessed on all construction projects financed by extra-budgetary funds from 1 October 1983. All extra-budgetary funds to be used on capital construction were also required to be deposited in the Construction Bank for half a year to a year before it could be released (Oksenberg and Tong, 1991).

for example, shrank from 25.7 percent in 1980 to 18.4 percent in 1987 (see the fourth column of Table 2.4). In addition, the central share of budgetary revenues kept shrinking since 1984[5] (see the last column of Table 2.5) because the central government had little collection machinery of its own before 1994. Most taxes and profits, whether they pertain to central, local or shared revenue source, had been collected by the local governments that did not have strong incentives to collect the shared revenues and even weaker to mobilize central revenue collection.

Table 2.5   Local extra-budgetary funds and national, central budgetary revenues, 1980–1993

	Local extra-budgetary funds (in billion *yuan*)	Local extra-budgetary funds/local budgetary revenues (%)	Total budgetary revenues/GDP (%)	Central budgetary revenue/national total (%)
1980	–	–	25.7	24.5
1981	–	–	24.2	26.5
1982	53.20	61.5	22.9	28.6
1983	60.78	69.3	23.0	35.8
1984	71.79	73.5	22.9	40.5
1985	89.39	72.4	22.4	38.4
1986	102.07	76.0	20.8	36.7
1987	120.08	82.1	18.4	33.5
1988	145.36	91.9	15.8	32.9
1989	158.66	86.1	15.8	30.9
1990	163.54	84.1	15.8	33.8
1991	186.22	84.2	14.6	29.8
1992	214.72	85.8	13.1	28.1
1993	118.66	35.0	12.6	22.0

Note: The scope of extra-budgetary funds was substantially narrowed in 1993.

Source: *Finance Yearbook of China*, various years.

---

5   The lack of central tax collection agency did not pose a challenge to the central share of budgetary revenues between 1982 and 1984 because the "Sichuan model" on which the fiscal scheme of 1980 was institutionalized was temporarily replaced in 1982 by "Jiangsu model" where all budgetary revenues were shared at a unanimous rate and was extended to most provinces except Guangdong and Fujian. However, when the fiscal scheme re-divided the revenues into the central, local and shared in 1985 and the shared revenues constituted a major portion of national budgetary revenue, the absence of central collection machinery made the central share of revenues quickly dropped from 40.5 percent in 1984 to 33.5 percent in just three years (see Table 2.4).

In 1988, a new fiscal system was implemented to raise budgetary, especially central budgetary, revenues. Six basic types of revenue-sharing scheme emerged as a result of a series of negotiations between the center and individual provinces (see Table 2.6). For ten province-level regions including provinces, minority autonomous regions, and municipalities directly under the central government as well as municipalities separately listed on the state plan, a specific rate of revenue growth was contracted with the center. Revenues within the range of that growth would be shared with the central government according to a fixed percentage determined on the basis of revenues and expenditures in 1987. Localities were allowed to retain all revenue above the contracted growth rate but needed to make up the gap between actual and expected central revenues if the growth rate fell below that contracted level. A simplified version of this arrangement was applied to Hunan and Guangdong where a growth rate rather than magnitude of revenue remittance was specified. More favorable treatment was awarded to Shanghai, Shandong and Heilongjiang where the amount of remittance had been a large proportion of their total revenues and the complaints were strongly voiced. The new system fixed their transfers to the center in absolute terms, so as to give them the full benefit of additional resource mobilization. Lastly, subsidies were fixed in absolute amounts for 16 deficit regions and the proportion of total revenues that should be remitted to the center were fixed for Tianjin, Anhui and Shanxi as well as three municipalities of Dalian, Qingdao and Wuhan.

Although provinces were strongly encouraged to mobilize their collection of revenues, the ratio of national budgetary revenues to GDP or that of central budgetary revenues to the national total (see the last two columns of Table 2.5) kept declining after 1988. The former was caused by the stipulation that provincial governments might generally retain greater share of the additional revenues beyond the contracted quota, which made the central share of revenues decrease at the margin. As a result, central revenues did not grow as fast as the national total. The reason for the declining ratio of national budgetary revenues to GDP was that the particular type of revenue-sharing schemes a province could get largely depended on its power of negotiation with the central government. Even when a specific scheme was agreed upon and would be fixed for five years, it still could be adjusted according to local economic conditions. For example, the remittance from Hunan province in 1990 was much less than contracted because they claimed that the centrally mandated agricultural price, subsidy price and wage policies had created expenditure pressures on their budget and they simply were unable to fulfill the contract. In other words, local governments would still "conceal revenues" to manipulate the distribution of revenues when the terms of the contract were not in their favor.

Table 2.6   The revenue sharing system of 1988

	Regions
1. Contracted rate of revenue growth	Beijing (4%); Hebei (4.5%), Henan (5%), Liaoning (3.5%), Jiangsu (5%), Zhejiang (6.5%); Shenyang (4%), Harbin (5%), Ningbo (5.3%), Chongqing (4%)
2. Contracted rate of remittance growth	Hunan (9%), Guangdong (7%)
3. Fixed amount of remittance	Shanghai (10.5), Shandong (0.29), Heilongjiang (0.3)
4. Fixed amount of subsidies	Jinlin (0.11), Jiangxi (0.05), Shanxi (0.12), Inner Mongolia (2.16), Gansu (0.13), Ningxia (0.59), Qinghai (0.74), Tibet (0.91), Xinjiang (1.76), Guizhou (0.90), Yunnan (0.71), Fujian (0.05), Guangxi (0.86), Hainan (0.14)
5. Uniform rate of remittance	Tianjin (53.5%), Shanxi (12.4%), Anhui (22.5%)
6. Progressive rate of remittance	Dalian (27.7% for within quota, 27.3% for beyond) Qingdao (16% and 34% respectively) Wuhan (17% and 25% respectively)

Note: Figures in parenthesis are the contracted rates (percent), remittance or subsidies (in billion *yuan*).

Source: Agarwala (1992).

2.2.2.2 Recentralized system in 1994

The failure of the 1988 fiscal scheme to improve the two ratios, namely, the ratio of the budgetary revenues to GDP and that of the central budgetary revenues to the national total, prompted the Third Plenary Session of the 14th of CCCPC to introduce a fundamental reform package called "tax assignment system" to address the problems inherent in all previous "fiscal responsibility systems" (CCCPC, 1993). First of all, this "tax assignment system," instead of a temporary fiscal arrangement that would be subject to periodic revision every few years, set up a long-standing intergovernmental fiscal relationship and made it unnecessary for the local states to conceal local budgetary revenue in expectation of more favorable terms in the next fiscal arrangement. The immediate consequence was the rising ratio of budgetary revenues to GDP immediately following the implementation of "tax assignment system." In addition, an independent set of collection machinery of central and shared taxes, National Taxation Bureaus (NTBs), was established in all provinces and cities in 1994 in order to secure the collection of central revenues. Taxes shared by the central and local governments would be collected by NTBs and a portion determined by the sharing rate would be returned to local governments. The local tax collection agency, Local Taxation Bureaus (LTBs), was only left with collecting local taxes.

Secondly, the fiscal system of 1994 redefined the sources of revenue for the central and local governments respectively on the basis of new tax categories (see Table 2.7),[6] which abruptly raised central share of budgetary revenue to around 50 percent since 1994. The general principle of tax revenue assignment between the central and local governments is that the taxes concerning national interests or macroeconomic management belonged to the central government while those related to local economic development were retained by local governments. In practice, however, the "tax assignment system" of 1994 and its subsequent

Table 2.7   Tax assignment system in 1994

	Tax categories
Central revenues	1. Customs duty 2. Consumption tax 3. Imported-related VAT collected at customs 4. Income tax of centrally owned SOEs 5. Taxes on banks, insurance companies and other financial institutions as well as taxes on railways (include business tax, income tax and urban maintenance and development tax)
Local revenues	1. Business tax, urban maintenance and development tax (except those of banks, insurance companies, other financial institutions and railways) 2. Income tax of locally owned SOEs 3. Personal income tax 4. Urban land use tax 5. Land value increment tax 6. Tax on the use of arable land 7. Building tax 8. Fixed asset investment adjustment tax 9. Agriculture and related taxes 10. Stamp tax 11. Animal slaughter tax
Shared revenues	1. VAT (the central 75%, local 25%) 2. Stamp tax on security exchange (half to half) 3. Resource tax

6   The industrial and commercial tax was replaced by VAT, consumption tax and business tax. VAT was levied on most manufactured goods at the uniform rate of 17 percent. Consumption tax was applied to luxury commodities such as cigarettes, alcohol, gasoline, diesel oil, automobile and cosmetics, while business tax was still used in sectors of transportation, construction, telecommunication and entertainment. The system also introduced land value increment tax, stamp tax on security exchange as well as legacy and gift tax and raised the rates of resource tax and urban maintenance and development tax. Besides, the previously differential corporate income tax rates for domestic SOEs, collective and private firms were consolidated into one uniform rate of 33 percent, while the personal income tax, personal income adjustment tax, and individual industrial and commercial household income tax were unified as the new personal income tax.

adjustments have been tailoring the revenue distribution toward the interests of the central government with increasing number of taxes to be shared with the center. For example, there were only 3 shared taxes among the total 30 tax categories in 1994 and they constituted 55 percent of national total budgetary revenues. When the number of tax categories became 22 in 2006, 8 of them had to be shared with the center and revenues collected from them took 72 percent of the national total. Besides, the sharing rates of individual taxes were also changed in favor of the central government. In May 1997, the central share of Stamp Tax on Security Exchange was changed from 50 to 88 percent and was gradually improved to 97 percent in October 2000. Starting from 2002, except for some special industries and companies (such as banking, China Gas Company, China Petroleum & Chemical Corporation), all EIT, regardless of the ownership of the enterprises, started to be shared with the center whose proportion increased from 50 percent in 2002 to 60 percent in 2003 (Su and Zhao, 2004).

Lastly, the central state has taken strict measures to institutionalize the extra-budgetary management since 1994 (Wong, 2001). For example, the General Rules on Enterprise Finance (*qi ye cai wu tong ze*) and Accounting Standards for Business Enterprises (*qi ye kuai ji zhun ze*) promulgated in November 1992 placed the enterprises post-tax profits under the direct supervision of the Ministry

Table 2.8   Local extra-budgetary funds and national, central budgetary revenues, 1993–2006

	Local extra-budgetary funds (in billion *yuan*)	Local extra-budgetary funds/ local budgetary revenues (%)	Total budgetary revenues/GDP (%)	Central budgetary revenue/national total (%)
1993	118.66	35.0	12.6	22.0
1994	157.92	68.3	10.8	55.7
1995	208.89	70.0	10.3	52.2
1996	294.57	78.6	10.4	49.4
1997	268.09	60.6	11.0	48.9
1998	291.81	58.6	11.7	49.5
1999	315.47	56.4	12.8	51.1
2000	357.88	55.9	13.5	52.2
2001	395.30	50.7	14.9	52.4
2002	403.90	47.4	15.7	55.0
2003	418.74	42.5	16.0	54.6
2004	434.85	36.6	16.5	54.9
2005	514.16	34.0	17.3	52.3
2006	594.08	32.5	18.4	52.8

Source: *Finance Yearbook of China*, various years.

of Finance, which made profits retained by enterprises less likely to be encroached upon by local governments (MOF, 1992a and 1992b). In September 1996, the State Council promulgated the Decision on Reinforcing the Management of Extra-budgetary Funds (*guo wu yuan guan yu jia qiang yu suan wai zi jin guan li de jue ding*) to shift 13 major governmental funds from the extra-budgetary account to the infra-budgetary one (State Council, 1996). More fundamentally, a comprehensive campaign of "transformation of administrative fees into taxes" (*fei gai shui*) was launched by premier Zhu Rongji in 1998. More than one fourth of items of fees were completely abolished. Most of the rest were transformed from irregular charges that were usually subject to the discretion of local states into the regular taxes that must fall under the surveillance of budgetary accounts. As a result of these major initiatives, the ratio of local extra-budgetary funds to local budgetary revenues (see the third column of Table 2.8) has been continuously declining since 1996.

2.2.2.3 Influx of FDI in the early 1990s
The immediate consequence of the fiscal system shift in 1994 was the influx of FDI and increasing pervasive FIEs that took the place of SOEs as the new generator of local economic and revenue growth. There had been far fewer FIEs in the 1980s than thereafter. As the dominating actor in Chinese economy during that decade, a number of SOEs were set up by the local governments across China so that the strategy of "concealing revenues" could be implemented with great ease. First of all, the illicit tax concession and ad hoc charges, instead of being an explicit formal contract between the local states and the enterprises they partnered, had to be based on a tacit mutual agreement between them. In other words, the enterprises were expected to voluntarily accept those mandatory charges as a return for the concessions in their tax liabilities, which, however, could hardly be accomplished by those without knowledge of this approach. As mentioned in Chapter 1, one of the major disadvantages FDI faces is its unfamiliarity with the cultural or political conditions of the host place. In case the FIEs turned out to be uncooperative on this matter, the hosting local governments would not only lose the revenues that could be collected if otherwise, but might also risk the exposure of this illicit approach. This strategy is also less applicable to central SOEs that were financially administered by the central government of China. In contrast, local SOEs would be a much more reliable partner than FIEs due to their close affiliation with the governments that set them up.

Secondly, local SOEs were generally much more tolerant than FIEs and private firms with respect to the aggressive governmental charges because they needed the protection of the local states from the uncertainty and competition in the market, the ecology called "soft budget constraint" (Kornai, 1990). The magnitude of these charges could be reflected by the fact that the ratio of the local extra-budgetary revenues to the budgetary revenues, as shown by the third column of Table 2.5, had been consistently increasing from 61.5 percent in 1982 to 91.9 percent in 1988, the implication of which was that an increasing share of enterprise profits was taken away by the local states. A stylized example may illustrate this point clearly. As presented in Table 2.9, suppose a local enterprise with the pre-tax profits of P in year zero. According to the rate of 55 percent, it should turn in the EIT of $0.55P$ and retain $0.45P$ post-tax profits. With the illicit tax concession by the local government, however, it is allowed a lower rate of 50 percent in year one, which means the enterprise retains the post-tax profits of $0.5P$. Then the ad hoc charge that goes toward extra-budgetary funds needs to be greater than $0.05P$ *yuan* so that the revenues collected by the local government can be raised. Suppose the charge is $0.1P$, which is equivalent to 20 percent both of the EIT and of the post-tax profits. Then enterprise will be left with $0.4P$ *yuan* profits. In year two, the tax rate remains 50 percent while the ratio of the ad hoc charge to the EIT rises to 25 percent, an assumption consistent with the observed pattern of extra-budgetary funds between 1982 and 1988. Under this circumstance, the governmental charge is $0.125P$ that is equal to 25 percent of the post-tax profits and the enterprise eventually will be left with the profits of only $0.375P$.

Table 2.9   Increasing ratio of extra-budgetary funds to budgetary revenues

	EIT	Post-EIT profits	Ratio of charges/EIT	Ad hoc charges	Retained profits
Year 0: 55% tax rate	$0.55\,P$	0.45 P	0	0	0.45 P
Year 1: 50% tax rate	$0.50\,P$	0.50 P	20%	0.1 P	0.4 P
Year 2: 50% tax rate	$0.50\,P$	0.50 P	25%	0.125 P	0.375 P

Note: In order to simplify the calculation, only the EIT that entirely belonged to the local governments is illustrated here. The conclusion based on this example, however, generally applies to other taxes such as VAT that were to be shared with the center at fixed rates.

The stylized example shows the profits eventually retained by the enterprise will decrease as long as the governmental charges, or more broadly speaking, the local extra-budgetary revenues, take an increasing share of the EIT, or local budgetary revenues, which is exactly what happened during the period from 1982 to 1988. The aggressiveness of governmental charges made the enterprise continuously worse off than they otherwise would be. Thus, it could be tolerated only by local SOEs because of their dependence on the local governments for tax allowances, credits at preferential terms, financial grants and commitment to take cover the losses (Ping, 2006). It was under such circumstances that in the 1980s and early 1990s SOEs proved to be a better partner of local governments than FIEs or private firms to sustain the growth of local extra-budgetary funds.

The role of SOEs in securing the financial strength of Chinese local states, however, was gradually replaced by the more competitive FIEs as a result of the fiscal recentralization. As mentioned before, the strategy of "concealing revenues" was no longer needed by the local states because the introduction of "tax assignment system" ruled out the expectation of the constant adjustment of fiscal schemes that had been based on the revenue and expenditure conditions of the previous few years. Consequently, SOEs were losing their significance as a critical player in the implementation of this strategy. Besides, the local states gained rather strong political and economic incentives to mobilize the collection of their budgetary revenue since 1994. Many of the SOEs set up before the 1990s, however, were under the reform of "grasping large enterprises and letting go of small enterprises" (*zhua da fang xiao*). A large number of small and medium-sized SOEs were offered for sale and large SOEs were subject to institutional restructuring (Wu, 2005). On the other hand, private firms in the early 1990s remained weak and small in general, which made them less eligible for the growth engine of budgetary revenues either. The only candidate was FIEs whose rise was ideologically supported by Deng Xiaoping's southern tour in 1992 and materially facilitated by those bold policies of opening as elaborated in the first chapter.

It should be noted that the first upsurge of FDI inflows occurred in 1992 (see Figure 1.1), two years before the "tax assignment system." The reason was the expectation of the "tax assignment system" before its nationwide institutionalization in 1994. The central government considered replacing the "fiscal responsibility system" with the "tax assignment system" as early as the Seventh Five-Year Plan (1986–1990) and it was already implemented in 1992 across nine pilot regions including the provinces of Zhejiang, Liaoning and Xinjiang as well as the municipalities of Tianjin, Shenyang, Dalian, Qindao, Wuhan and Chongqing. These initiatives convinced local states that "fiscal responsibility system" would be replaced by the new "tax assignment system" in no time. That expectation not only made them less interested in "concealing revenues," but also strongly motivated the localities to mobilize their revenue collection as 1994 was approaching because of the guarantee by the central government that any gap between the local budgetary revenue in 1994 and that in 1993 would be filled by the central-to-local transfers (see section 2.3). One illustration of such efforts was the rampant sprawl of "development zones" as described in Chapter 1. As a result, local budgetary revenues reached 434.9 billion *yuan* in 1993, significantly higher than 314.9 billion *yuan* in 1991 and 348.3 billion *yuan* in 1992.

2.3 Implications of Fiscal Recentralization for Local State Entrepreneurialism

In addition to its immediate impact on the local demand for FDI, the recentralized "tax assignment system" also generated long-standing imperatives for local states to mobilize revenue collection, especially from manufacturing and real estate. Firstly, central fiscal strength is significantly improved at the expense of the local. According to the principle of public finance that the scope of expenditure should be matched with available revenues for each level of government, the expenditure responsibilities of the central and local states should also be divided in line with the tax revenues they are entitled to. The central state was supposed to shoulder an increasing share of national expenditure when the proportion of the central budgetary revenues in the national total was raised from 22 percent in 1993 to 55.7 percent in 1994 (see the last column of Table 2.8). Unlike the clear division of revenues, however, the expenditure coverage of the central and local states was not explicitly specified in the "tax assignment system" of 1994. As China has maintained a centralized political system where local government plays a much less active role in shaping the central decision-making than those in many other decentralizing systems (Bardhan, 2002), many duties were simply assigned to the local states via political fiats without corresponding support revenues (Wong, 2000).

The asymmetry between local revenues and expenditures was further aggravated in 1995 when the primary objective of the SOE reform switched from "power delegating and profits sharing" to "grasping large enterprises and letting go of small enterprises." Many small and medium-sized SOEs were either transformed into enterprises of other ownerships via merger, leasing, contracting, and offering for sale or simply became bankrupt and went into liquidation. In order to prevent social chaos, local states were instructed to take over the primary responsibilities for a wide range of social services in education, child and health care and pensions that SOEs used to provide to their employees. That abruptly raised their expenditure without the support of corresponding revenue sources (Ma and Norregaard, 2000). The gap between local budgetary revenue and expenditure rose steadily along with the progress of Chinese economic reform (see Figure 2.1).

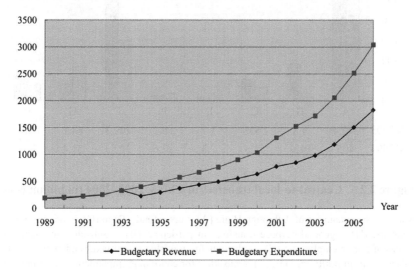

Figure 2.1   Budgetary revenues and expenditures of Chinese local governments, 1989–2006 (in billion Chinese *yuan*)

Source: *China Statistical Yearbook*, 2007.

Secondly, local governments have to count on the central-to-local fiscal transfers to finance their expanding expenditures because they are generally forbidden by the Budget Law (NPC, 1994) to incur domestic or foreign debts. In fact, the total indirect and implicit local borrowing from government employees and commercial banks was estimated to be over 1,000 billion *yuan* by the end of 2004 (Zheng, 2008). The magnitude a locality may receive in the transfers, however, depends to a large extent on the incremental VAT and EIT it collects. There are three broad categories of transfer programs (see Figure 2.2). The first one is regular "tax refund". As the "tax assignment system" would certainly reduce the revenues at the local level, most provinces that had benefited from the fiscal scheme effective between 1988 and 1993 did not comply. The center then had to recognize the vested interests of local governments by guaranteeing that each locality retained no less than what it had in 1993. In addition, 30 percent of the incremental central revenue collected from VAT and consumption tax would be returned to the local governments as reward for revenue collection, which meant

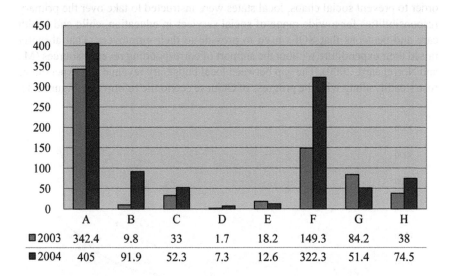

	A	B	C	D	E	F	G	H
■2003	342.4	9.8	33	1.7	18.2	149.3	84.2	38
■2004	405	91.9	52.3	7.3	12.6	322.3	51.4	74.5

Figure 2.2   Central-to-local transfers in China, 2003–2004 (in billion *yuan*)

Note: 1. The categories of A through H are (A) = tax refund; (B) to (G) = specific-purpose transfers; (H) = general-purpose transfers. In particular, (B) = Subsidies for increasing wages of public employees; (C) = subsidies for abolishing rural taxes and charges; (D) = subsidies for minority regions; (E) = subsidies for continuing implementation of pre-1994 fiscal schemes; (F) = earmarked grants; (G) = other specific-purpose transfers. 2. Tax refund does not include the local portion of shared tax revenues.

Source: Shah and Shen (2006).

51 percent of the incremental VAT would be received by the local governments.[7] In 2002, a similar scheme was instituted for personal income tax and EIT. Provinces would receive no less than what they had in 2001 from both taxes and a certain proportion of the incremental tax revenues would be refunded by the center.

The second broad category of transfer payment includes various specific-purpose subsidies and grants, such as the subsidies for increasing wages of public employees, abolishing rural taxes and charges, minority regions, and the continuing implementation of pre-1994 fiscal schemes as well as more than 200 "earmarked grants" that are used to support projects of education provision, environmental protection, agricultural improvement, the health service and disaster relief. Because a dominating majority of the specific-purpose transfers are grants whose distributions are usually determined at the discretion of the supervising central ministries at Beijing, "*pao bu qian jin*" or "visiting officials of central departments for grants" become a common phenomenon for the localities in competition for them. It was estimated that the number of "*zhu jing ban*" or "representative offices" at Beijing that were established by local governments, large SOEs, universities and research institutions for their lobbying activities was beyond 10,000 (Guo, 2008). The last category of the central-to-local transfer payment is the "transitional transfers" (renamed "general-purpose transfers" in 2002) that are intended to narrow the disparities of the general financial capacity across different regions. Its proportion among all central-to-local transfers, however, has been less than 10 percent since 1994, which led to a growing regional disparity in public service delivery (World Bank, 2005).

The gap between local budgetary revenues and expenditures as well as the structure of central-to-local transfers strongly motivated the local states to mobilize their revenue collection, especially from business tax, VAT and EIT. On the one hand, these three taxes have much broader tax bases than most other tax categories and greater importance is attached to them by local governments in China (see Table 2.10). Business tax and VAT are levied on most service sectors and manufacturing industries respectively while EIT is collected from all profitable businesses. In 2006, the fourth largest source of local tax revenue was personal income tax with the contribution of 98.2 billion *yuan*, far below the revenues raised from EIT. Since the growth of manufacturing and real estate demands much less time and effort from local governments than the success of advanced service sectors does, promoting their prosperity is a more cost-efficient approach for localities to significantly increase local budgetary revenues within the limited office terms. On the other hand, the "tax refund" is institutionally more reliable than the "specific-purpose transfers" and quantitatively much greater than

---

7   According to the 30:70 rate of sharing, the local governments were allowed the 30 percent of the incremental VAT in the first place. In addition, they will be returned the 30 percent of those belonging to the central government, which is 21 percent of the whole incremental VAT. Thus, the total share of the incremental VAT that can be retained by the local government is 30+21=51 percent.

the "general-purpose transfers." As the magnitude of this most important central-to-local transfer program depends on the incremental VAT and EIT to a great extent, the continuing growth of the manufacturing sector on which the VAT and EIT are levied is critical to the amount of transfer a locality may receive from the central government.

Table 2.10   Composition of local budgetary revenue, 2002–2006 (in billion yuan)

	Budgetary revenue				
	Tax revenue				Non-tax revenue
	Total	Business tax	VAT	EIT	
2002	740.62	229.50	154.74	120.06	110.88
2003	841.32	276.76	181.10	117.88	143.67
2004	999.96	347.10	240.44	159.60	189.38
2005	1272.67	410.28	286.08	213.99	237.40
2006	1523.36	496.82	319.64	268.11	88.05

Source: *Finance Yearbook of China*, 2007.

Chapter 3
Growth of Urban Real Estate Sector

The stringent state regulation in the mid 1990s cooled off the over-heated Chinese economy. China's FDI inflows plummeted to the lowest point in 1999 (see Figure 1.1). So did the adjusted "investment index" that measures its involvement in Chinese manufacturing industries (see Table 1.2). From the start of this century, however, FDI regained momentum with quickly rising contracted inflows and "size index" as well as "investment index" significantly higher than those of other countries. Because the strength of Chinese domestic firms had been admittedly improved since the overhauling reform of SOEs in the late 1990s, this resurging dynamics of FDI suggests the dependence of the Chinese manufacturing sector on FDI, especially on those cross-border investments with considerable magnitudes of investments, was well maintained by factors other than the simple substitute for insolvent SOEs as elaborated in Chapter 2.

Perhaps one of the major domestic institutional changes around the turn of the century was the intertwined urban housing and land use reforms that generated far-reaching impacts. The coincidence between it and FDI dynamics as outlined above prompts investigation of their causal relationship. This chapter and the next jointly present the role of urban land use regime in shaping the municipal demand for FDI. Specifically, this chapter examines how the intertwined urban housing and land use reforms that were initiated from the end of the 1990s enabled entrepreneurial local states to stimulate urban real estate development by driving up the price of land intended for residential or commercial uses. Chapter 4, on the other hand, presents how municipalities woo prospective investors with excessively low prices of land for manufacturing production. Given finite land resource that is being made increasingly scarce by the relentless acquisition of municipalities, such contrasting land pricing strategies strongly motivates the preference of local states for manufacturing FDI that demonstrates generally higher land use intensity.

3.1 Urban Housing Provision and Land Use before 1998

Sustained growth of the urban real estate sector has to be supported by substantive demand for housing units on one hand and a market-based urban land market on the other, both of which, however, were absent from Chinese cities before 1998 when the state had been extensively involved in urban housing provision and land development. This section examines major initiatives to reform the socialist housing and urban land use systems between 1978 and 1998 and discusses how they failed to generate housing demand or establish a well-institutionalized land use scheme, which prompted the comprehensive marketization of urban housing and land provision in 1998.

3.1.1 Reforming Urban Housing Provision

In the pre-reform socialist China, urban housing had been financed by state investments and directly provided by SOEs to their employees at extremely low rents. Measures such as increasing rents or selling stock housing, however, still had to be heavily subsidized by SOEs. The consequence was little demand for housing on the market and slow urban real estate development during the two decades.

3.1.1.1 Free housing provision in pre-reform socialist China

Before 1978, about 60 percent of urban housing units had been provided by SOEs as part of the socialist welfare package with the rest developed by the local governments as public housing for workers in small-sized enterprises that were ineligible for state investments and could not afford to build by themselves (Wu, 1995). Housing investments were planned along with other capital construction investments by the state for individual SOEs. It is those receiving SOEs which were responsible for the whole process of land development, physical construction and housing distribution. In a socialist state where industrial production was prioritized over collective consumption, such a project-specific approach to develop urban housing proved to be effective in minimizing the cost of labor reproduction so that the scarce financial resources could be concentrated on the production-oriented industrialization, which was exemplified by the rise of "factory towns" in the period of three-front construction when key industrial projects as well as housing units were relocated to hinterland regions for the sake of military security.

The financial dependence on state investments, however, caused serious difficulty in sustaining housing provision. In order to symbolize the socialist ideology of proletarianism as well as its superiority over capitalist competitors, almost all urban housing stock was leased by SOEs to their workers at extremely low rates that had remained intact for a long time. For example, the average monthly rent was still 0.13 *yuan* for each square meter in 1987 when the maintenance cost was about *2 yuan* (Fong, 1988) and the construction costs reached 177 *yuan* for each square meter of floor space in 1985 (Kwok, 1986). The provision of housing units then became a heavy burden to the socialist state because it was impossible to cover the construction and maintenance costs with mere state money and negligible rent. As a result, urban housing received decreasing amounts of state investment with the average urban living space per person shrinking from 45 square meters before 1952 to 3.6 in 1979 (Li, 1999). It was a quite ubiquitous housing phenomenon across Chinese cities in the late 1970s that a three-generation family of five members had to be squeezed into a flat of 25 square meters. The immediate solution to such inadequate urban housing provision that plagued the state financially and most residents physically was to raise the rent by a wide margin and/or sell housing stocks to their current dwellers in an extensive way.

3.1.1.2 Increasing rents and selling housing stocks, 1978–1997

Apart from the financial constraint, the housing problem was further complicated by the rapidly increasing urban population that grew from 57.65 million in 1949 to 172.45 million in 1979. In view of the urban population pressure and the unsustainable financial architecture, Deng Xiaoping, the chief architect of China's reform and openness policy, gave an important talk on 2 April 1980 to central leaders:

> Urban residents may either buy or build houses. Both new and old houses can be sold and both outright purchase and installment over 10 to 15 years are acceptable. When the sale program starts, rent may have to be upward adjusted in accordance with the house sale price so that buying worth more than renting. It should also vary on the basis of the location of house. Low wage worker should be subsidized when the rent increases. All these aspects should be taken into account. (Deng, 1980)

Although this statement did not explicitly use terms like "commercialization" or "marketization," the proposed ideas of "house sale," "rent adjustment" as well as "subsidies" actually announced the switch of urban housing provision from socialist welfare solely financed by the state to market-based commodity whose costs should be distributed among the state, SOEs and individuals.

In 1982, a pilot experiment was carried out in four cities of Changzhou, Zhengzhou, Siping and Shashi where state employees could purchase the houses they occupied at one third of the total price and the other two-thirds were evenly split between the SOEs the buyers were affiliated with and the municipal governments. The "soft budget constraint" of SOEs as discussed in the last chapter, however, enabled the latter to transfer the housing subsidies they should pay to SOEs eventually (Jia and Liu, 2007). As a result, the more houses were sold, the heavier the burden on SOEs selling them, which made them reluctant to participate in this program. On the other hand, since it was a heavily subsidized sale program, buyers were not allowed to resell the properties they purchased to a third party at market prices. That restriction made this program much less appealing to prospective buyers, especially those with middle and high incomes who would like full property rights. Consequently, most employees still chose to live in the residential units provided by the SOEs at low rents. Due to lack of support on both sides of sellers and buyers, this sale program that was once extended to over 160 cities had to be ended in 1985.

In 1986, a Housing Reform Leading Team (*zhu fang gai ge ling dao xiao zu*) consisting of representatives from a wide range of ministries was established to address the problems left over by the previous housing program. The immediate objectives involved raising low rent, introducing housing subsidies as well as encouraging house purchase completely paid by individuals. Yantai, Tangshan and Bangbu were selected as the pilot cities. Yantai proposed a new average monthly rent of 1.28 *yuan* per square meter that was a significant rise over the original rent of 0.13 *yuan*. Depending on the location, size and quality of the housing unit, the particular rent each family needed to pay varied around that average level. Under the new scheme, a large proportion of direct costs caused by construction and maintenance and indirect expenses such as management expenditures and interest associated with investments could be covered by the rents. In the meantime, subsidies were provided by SOEs with the amount of a fixed proportion of wages to make housing affordable to most employees. Tenants were also encouraged to buy the housing units they occupied. Preferential sale prices were proposed. A minimum of 30 percent down payment was required with discounts granted to higher percentages and the remainder to be paid against mortgage loans over 10 to 20 years.

In 1988, the housing reform in Yantai was officially endorsed by the 1st national housing reform conference that promulgated the Implementation Plan to Practice Urban Housing System Reform by Stages and in Batches (State Council, 1988a). Nationwide housing reform program, however, was delayed by the rising inflation in late 1988 and the political unrest in June 1989. The halt continued till 1991 when the resolution of the 2nd national housing reform conference, Circular on Promoting Comprehensive Urban Housing Reform, required all municipalities develop housing reform plans in accordance with the principle of increasing rents and selling houses (State Council, 1991). Specifically, it suggested "more increase and fewer subsidies" (*duo ti shao bu*) so that the existing tenants could be pushed to purchase the housing units they currently occupied. It also specified the market prices and standard prices at which SOEs should sell their housing stocks to their employees. As the land used by SOEs for housing construction was usually acquired through state assignment for free, standard prices were based on the construction expenses only but excluded land costs. Housing units which were sold at standard prices were not permitted to be circulated on the open market, whereas buyers had full property rights over those sold at higher market prices.

3.1.1.3 Involvement of SOEs in housing provision

The reform program, however, did not achieve the intended objective. First of all, the initiative of "more increase and fewer subsidies" received strong objections from communist cadres who would have to pay more for the larger houses they occupied. To compromise, the amount of subsidies had to be improved in proportion to the rent increase. In 1992, the nationwide housing subsidies reached 97.13 billion *yuan*, more than 10 times of the 6.9 billion *yuan* in 1979 (Wu, 1996). Secondly, heavy rent subsidies not only heavily burdened SOEs, they also made house purchase a less worthy option for existing tenants. As a result, many SOEs had to sell the residential units that were financed by state investments to their employees at rates substantially below the standard prices. In 1988, for example, the national average sale price for each square meter of existing houses was only

65.7 *yuan* (Jia and Liu, 2007) while the market price was 703 *yuan* in 1990 (Wang and Murie, 1999).

In addition to the fire sale of existing housing stocks, some SOEs, especially those large-sized ones, also bought new housing units from the market and resold them to their employees at much lower prices. In the early 1990s, state capital was no longer the only source of investment in housing provision. An increasing number of real estate companies participated in urban housing development with more than 23,000 real estate companies operating in China at the end of 1995 (Wang and Murie, 1999). A majority of those newly built residential units, however, was bought by large SOEs instead of by individuals. In 1995, only less than half of the new residential units were directly sold to individuals (Wang and Murie, 1999). This proportion dropped to one third in 1996 (Cheng, 1999). Besides, because land used by many SOEs was assigned by the state free of charge, some SOEs usually requested more than needed and eventually used those spaces to build housing projects for their employees with the prices only half of the prevailing market rates or even less (Wang, Wang et al., 2005).

The benefits associated with these housing provisions accrued only to employees in large SOEs and state organs that either had adequate financial strength to purchase housing units from the market or had spare land that was allocated for free to conduct housing construction. The reason for their continuing involvement in subsidizing housing provision was the "soft budget constraint" they had been under. The fire sale of housing units could disproportionally benefit the leaders of SOEs who usually occupied larger houses but had not been held truly accountable for the financial conditions of the SOEs. The sale of new housing units would win them wider support from the regular workers who could get more spacious residential units at prices substantially below the market levels. In contrast, most of the small or medium-sized SOEs, private firms or FIEs were ineligible for state investments in housing construction and had no housing stocks to be sold to their employees. Without generous support from the enterprises they were affiliated with, employees of these firms had to purchase houses from market. When the housing price surged up in the early 1990s as a result of land speculations, many of them could not afford residential units sold on the market and increasing numbers of newly built houses became empty (Wang and Murie, 1999).

In order to help people finance their housing purchases, the 3rd national housing reform conference in 1993 proposed the establishment of "housing provident fund" by drawing upon the successful comprehensive housing reform plan launched in Shanghai in 1991. In addition to the programs of rent increase and housing subsidies as well as sale of houses, Shanghai's plan required both employees and employers to contribute 5 percent of wages toward individual accounts deposited in an interest-earning and tax-free housing provident fund. The percentage rate was later adjusted upward to 7 percent in accordance with rising personal incomes and market housing prices. Intended to secure financial sources that could be used to purchase houses from the market and free SOEs from heavy subsidies, this saving could be used only for major housing-related expenditures such as purchases and could be withdrawn only upon retirement if otherwise. Given its function to improve the purchasing power of individual house buyers, the proposal to establish the provident fund was officially adopted in 1994 by the State Council's Decision on Deepening Urban Housing System Reform (State Council, 1994). Unfortunately, partly because of the insufficient balances in the housing provident fund and partly due to the lack of strict regulations against subsidized house sales by large SOEs, the demand for housing on the market had remained weak until 1998.

3.1.2 Reforming Urban Land Use Schemes

Like the pre-reform urban housing provision system where the construction of residential units was financed by the state and provided to the workers as part of the welfare package, all urban land had been owned by the state and distributed to users free of charge. Reform initiatives that injected market mechanism into the socialist scheme, however, preserved state assignment as a means to grant LURs (LURs). That exclusively favored those developers who had close affiliations with the municipal governments while largely discouraging private investments in urban real estate development.

3.1.2.1 Pre-1978 urban land use

The state ownership of land was institutionalized soon after the founding of China in 1949 and has remained intact since then. It was first practiced in the rural areas with the Land Reform Act of 1950 stipulating that rural land property owned by landlords be confiscated via collectivization and redistributed to rural households according to headcount as well as the quality of land parcel (Central People's Government, 1950). The rationale was that the rent of land was derived from exploitation of surplus labor in production and should be eliminated in a socialist country. In line with this rural land reform, the private ownership of urban land was gradually replaced by state ownership through the socialist transformation (*she hui zhu yi gai zao*) of urban private properties since 1949. Article 10 of the Suburban Land Reform Ordinance promulgated in 1950 stipulated that all suburban land acquired or confiscated from agricultural uses was owned by the state and managed by the municipal governments (State Council, 1950). In 1956, the CCPCC announced its Opinions on the Basic Conditions of Current Urban Private Property and Its Socialist Transformation according to which all urban vacant land and road land occupied by private owners should be confiscated by the state via appropriate approaches (CCPCC, 1956). As Zhang (1997) noted, virtually all private land in China had been converted into state ownership by 1953.

Aside from its public ownership, socialist urban land scheme was also characterized by the free-of-charge state assignment and non-transferability. First of all, urban land was administratively allocated by the state to SOEs according to the assigned production plan. In a production-oriented command system, this was believed to achieve rational distribution of resources via economic planning. Land speculation and land-based labor exploitation would no longer be possible as a result of such free state allocation. Secondly, transfer of land titles between users was prohibited on the ground that market transactions would disturb the static state assignment process and make actual land use as well as production deviate from the original plan. The absence of market mechanisms, however, meant the urban land use was not based on price principle through which different actors might bid for the use of properties according to the benefits they could expect from their operations at that particular location. Consequently, this system of free assignment of urban land by the state led to land use inefficiencies in urban areas. Because industrial production was given the highest priority by the state, industrial land was usually located in urban cores while residential land was squeezed out. For example, more than 20 percent of the total land in the central area of Shanghai and more than 30 percent in that of Guangzhou was used for industrial production (Yang and Liu, 1991). Bertaud and Renaud (1992) also found similar land use pattern across other socialist cities.

3.1.2.2 Levying land use fees, 1979–1986
Urban land use reform remained largely intact as China launched ground-breaking reforms in a wide range of economic fields in the late 1970s. The reason for delay of change in this particular aspect was the potential social instability and political uncertainty associated with privatizing public urban land. Not only had the private land tenure system been deemed against the fundamental ideology of socialism, it might also leave the state with fewer resources and instruments to exert its control over urban economic growth. The infeasibility of land privatization, however, did not mean problems inherent in the socialist urban land use could not be addressed at all via other forms of institutional shift. The general solution, as summarized by the announcement of 14th CCP National Congress in 1992 that explicitly set the establishment of socialist market economy as the goal of China's reform, was to inject a capitalist market mechanism into the economic arena whilst maintaining socialist rule in the political sphere at the same time. It was on the basis of such general policy orientation that private use rights was separated from public ownership and paid land use and market-based transferability became the objectives of urban land reform in China.

The initial reform attempt in urban land use arose from the entry of FDI following the opening policy of China. In the late 1970s and early 1980s, it was financially difficult for most municipalities to prepare serviced land or build urban physical infrastructure to attract foreign investments. Paid land use, however, was prohibited by Constitution that explicitly stipulated "no organization or individual may seize, buy, sell, lease land or make any other unlawful transfer of land" (NPC, 1982). In 1979, the city of Guangzhou negotiated with Hong Kong investors with the condition that the latter bore the land development costs and provided off-site urban infrastructure. This approach to exchange LURs for capital investment in urban construction was quickly endorsed by the Sino-Foreign Equity Joint Venture Law that required a land use fee be charged to the joint venture if the land parcel was not used by the Chinese partners as capital input (NPC, 1979). In accordance with this law, Shenzhen introduced Interim Provisions on land Management in Shenzhen Special Economic Zone in 1982 to start levying annual land use fees with the rate ranging from 1 to 21 *yuan* per square meter depending on the specific location (People's Congress of Guangdong Province, 1982). In the following five years, 82 square kilometers of land had been acquired through the municipal government of Shenzhen among which 17 square kilometers were levied a total of 40 million *yuan* land use fees. By the mid 1980s, one third of all Chinese cities levied the land use fees on a differential basis (Ma, 1992) to finance urban infrastructure construction.

Intense competition between localities for inward investment usually made land use fees too low to reflect the real market value of urban land. Consequently, urban land use pattern remained inefficient. In 1985, the acreage of arable land decreased by 1 million hectares as a result of aggressive land acquisition, which was the largest annual loss since 1949 (Zhang, 1997). In November 1988, the Tentative Ordinance of PRC on Urban Land Use Tax substituted uniform land use tax for the land use fees that had been determined entirely at the discretion of municipalities (State Council, 1988b). Most urban land users including Chinese domestic firms but excluding governments, civic groups, armies and religious entities were required to pay an annual land use tax between 0.5 to 10 *yuan* per square meter in big cities, 0.4 to 8 *yuan* in middle-sized cities, 0.3 to 6 *yuan* in small cities and 0.2 to 4 *yuan* in towns. These regulated rates, however, were adjusted upwards only once in 2007 and quickly lagged behind the constantly rising land values as a result of that rigidity. That localities were allowed to set their own rates within these already out-of-date ranges left them great latitude in picking the low extremes to please investors.

Besides, when the Chinese partner in a joint venture used the land they originally occupied as their capital input, its value was usually underestimated. That was then translated into the undervaluation of the assets invested by the Chinese partner. Thus most of the benefits generated by such joint ventures were collected by the actual users of land, especially foreign investors, rather than by the ultimate owner, the state. That problem, as well as the inefficient land use pattern, had to be solved in a free urban land market where the price of land is not determined by administrative assessment but through land transactions. It is under these circumstances that China adopted a land use system resembling the leasehold scheme of Hong Kong (Chan, 1999). That is, LURs could be leased from the state and transferred between users in the land market with the ownership still belonging to the state.

3.1.2.3 Involvement of local states in granting LURs, 1988–1997

The first case of leasing LURs to private developers took place at Shenzhen on 9 September 1987 as soon as pilot reform in this field was approved at six coastal cities of Shenzhen, Guangzhou, Xiamen, Fuzhou, Shanghai and Tianjin. A domestic company based in Shenzhen obtained the use right of a 5,322 square meters parcel of land for 50 years at *negotiated* price of 200 *yuan* per square meter. On 25 November, an area of 46,355 square meters planned for residential housing was sold to another company through *tender* at the price of 368 *yuan* per square meter. A few days later, the first *auction*-based LURs transfer occurred on 1 December with 8,588 square meters residential land leased out at 611 *yuan* per square meter. On the basis of these experiments with LURs transactions, the Constitution of PRC was amended in April 1988 with the added clause that "the LURs may be transferred in accordance with the law," which marked a fundamental ideological breakthrough in establishing a legal framework of urban land market. Accordingly, the Land Management Law of PRC was amended in December 1988 with the stipulation that "the LURs of state-owned or collective-owned land may be transferred in accordance with the law" and "the state adopts a paid land use system for state-owned land" (NPC, 1988).

On the implementation level, the detailed methods of urban land transactions were legislated in May 1990 by the Provisional Regulation on Granting and Transferring LURs of Urban State-Owned Land, abbreviated as "land use regulation" hereafter (State Council, 1990b). According to this regulation, urban land transactions involved three separate but interlinked phases. The first phase referred to the municipal acquisition of agricultural land that belonged to the rural collectives. Any direct transactions between prospective urban users and existing farmers were prohibited with the land title certificate only being issued by the local branches of State Land Administration Bureau. Once the land was acquired and became ready for development, it entered the second phase or the primary land market where the LURs of newly acquired land were granted (*chu rang*)[1] by the state to the users at prices determined through negotiation, tender auction or quotation. Specifically, negotiation was conducted in a private manner between local governments and developers. Tender and auction were more transparent in that both sought competition among prospective users. The tender which matched the publicly set criteria and had recognized advantages over the competitors got the LURs and the highest bidder in an auction won it. In 2002, a fourth means of "quotation" was added to the existing methods of negotiation, tender and auction to grant LURs. It meant the terms for land use were published by municipal government in the first place, followed by public quotations from bidders for at least 10 days. The winner was the one who offered the highest price at the end of this period. Since the tax assignment system was implemented in 1994, the premium paid by the land users for LURs they received could be entirely retained by municipal governments and became another major local revenue source in addition to the budgetary revenue and extra-budgetary funds. The third phase of urban land transaction was characterized by the transfer (*zhuan rang*) of

---

1   The word "grant" is the English translation of the Chinese term *chu rang* as used by most law firms in Hong Kong. It means the state, owner of all urban land, sells the LURs to users in the market.

LURs between users or other land circulation activities such as rental or collateral conducted by the land users in the secondary land market.

The market-oriented "land use regulation," however, did not completely abolish the conventional land assignment system. It was still reserved as an important tool in the hands of the state to maintain the social and economic order and avoid the destructive impacts brought about by the radical "shock therapy" as occurred in East European countries. Such an institutional setting, or a dual-track system, made it tremendously profitable to get the LURs via state assignment or at negotiated prices on the one hand and re-sell them later to others at much higher market rates on the other (Yeh and Wu, 1996). Table 3.1 shows that the approach of state assignment (denoted by "2") was adopted in more than 70 percent of all cases to grant LURs in the mid 1990s as opposed to only 15 percent in the mid 2000s. Furthermore, among those conducted via negotiation, tender, auction and quotation (denoted by "1"), private negotiation, the mode of land sale that involved the least transparent land transactions between the state as owner and the developers as users, dominated throughout the 1990s. For example, nearly 90 percent of the cases to grant LURs were the outcomes of the under-the-table negotiations in 1998 (Ho and Lin, 2003). That proportion, however, was only around 70 percent in the 2000s.

Table 3.1   **Granting LURs via market pricing and administrative assignment, 1994–1995 and 2004–2006**

		1994	1995	2004	2005	2006
Negotiation, tender and auction (1)	Cases (no.)	42,076	105,473	184,850	162,112	186,667
	Acreage (ha.)	57,338	43,092	181,510	165,586	233,018
State assignment (2)	Cases (no.)	166,690	292,285	36,844	30,581	30,747
	Acreage (ha.)	89,750	87,608	62,054	64,623	63,791
$\frac{(1)}{(1)+(2)}$	Cases (%)	20.1	26.5	83.4	84.1	85.9
	Acreage (%)	40.0	33.0	74.5	71.9	78.5

Note: Data for 2004 and 2005 includes those granted via quotation.

Source: China Statistical Yearbook, 1995–1996; *China Land and Resources Almanac*, 2005–2007.

The privileges associated with receiving LURs via state or negotiation instead of market mechanisms, however, were only limited to quasi-governmental developers that had close affiliation with municipal governments. Although it was generally forbidden by the "land use regulation" to transfer or lease those LURs to another user to make profits, exceptions were made in circumstances under which such transactions were approved by municipal government and the original users turned in the full revenues collected from the transfers of LURs. Unfortunately, that policy against cross-track land speculation was not strictly enforced in practice. In some cases, municipal governments received only 10 percent of the transfer revenues from the original users (Ye, 2005). As a result of the continuing state involvement in granting LURs, many private investments in urban real estate development that did not have substantive connections to local governments were crowded out and urban land use inefficiencies as represented by the proximity of private commercial land uses to the sites for education, military and transportation purposes (Yeh and Wu, 1996) remained largely intact.

3.2 Market-Oriented Urban Housing and Land Use Reforms in 1998

As illustrated before, housing provision by SOEs diminished the housing demand on the market, and granting LURs at the discretion of the state crowded out private investments in housing production. Consequently, the development of the real estate sector became slow and weak by the end of the last century. More importantly, state involvement in both fields caused great inequalities by exclusively benefiting those affiliated with the state. All these entailed more fundamental reforms to improve urban housing and land use conditions by promoting real estate development.

3.2.1 Marketization of Housing Provision

The initiatives to terminate the involvement of SOEs in housing provision was prompted by the Asian financial crisis in 1997. The shrinking demands of those affected countries for labor-intensive consumption goods posed great challenges to the economic growth of China that had been largely driven by investments and exports. That was even aggravated by the depreciated currencies of major Southeast countries such as Thailand, Indonesia, Malaysia, and Philippine, which made the export-led industries of China less competitive in the international arena. According to Chinese official statistics, 4.3 percent of China's GDP was contributed by its net export in 1997 while the proportion dropped to only 2.7 percent in 1999 (SSB, 2008a). A series of expansionary monetary and fiscal policies was implemented to stimulate the growth of domestic consumption and investment. For example, the deposit reserve ratio for commercial banks was lowered from 13 percent in March 1998 to 6 percent in November 1999 to encourage private investments and investments in capital construction projects by the state increased from approximately 52 billion *yuan* 1996 to 147 billion *yuan* in 1999.

It was in this context that urban housing was selected as the critical investment and consumption area to sustain economic growth. Following the 4th national housing reform conference, the State Council promulgated the Circular on Further

Deepening Urban Housing Reform and Expediting Housing Construction (State Council, 1998) in July 1998. For the first time since 1978, this document explicit posited marketized housing provision as a "new economic growth engine." One of the most critical changes it introduced was to substitute a commodity-based housing system where individual households would finance their house purchases with private savings, provident funds and housing mortgages for the welfare housing provision by SOEs and state organs that have been prevailing for decades. That was expected to significantly boost housing demand on the market by forcing those who had not received housing provisions from the SOEs or state organs to purchase or rent residential units from the open market.

In the meantime, the People's Bank of China (PBC) promulgated the Management Measures on Individual Housing Mortgages (PBC, 1998) that released the cap on the aggregate number of mortgages a commercial bank was allowed to issue. In order to encourage applications for housing mortgages, the down payment could be 30 percent of the total price, the repayment period was extended to 20 years and the interest rates of installments were set to be lower than those for the regular bank loans of the same terms. As a result of these measures, nationwide balances of housing mortgages rocketed from 19 billion *yuan* (0.25 percent of all loan balances) in 1997, through 740 billion *yuan* (5.89 percent of bank loan balances) in 2002, to 1,840 billion *yuan* (9.45 percent of all loan balances) at the end of 2005 (Wang, 2006; PBC, 2006). Together with the growing provident savings, the rising mortgages greatly improved the purchasing power of individual households. The floor areas of sold ordinary housing units that have been the largest category of residential buildings increased from 122 million meter squares in 2000 to 484 million 2006 (see Table 3.2).

Table 3.2   Floor areas of sold commodity buildings, 2000–2006 (in hectares)

	Residence			Office	Commerce	Others
	Ordinary	Luxurious	Affordable			
2000	12,169.49	640.72	3,760.07	436.98	1,399.31	230.56
2001	15,039.09	878.19	4,021.47	502.57	1,696.15	274.44
2002	18,457.44	1,241.26	4,003.61	538.92	2,218.58	348.47
2003	24,310.11	1,449.87	4,018.87	630.49	2,833.10	475.19
2004	28,235.04	2,323.05	3,261.80	692.84	3,100.29	618.62
2005	43,564.38	2,818.44	3,205.01	1,096.23	4,081.38	720.78
2006	48,413.54	3,672.44	3,336.97	1,231.04	4,337.79	865.29

Source: *China Statistical Yearbook*, various years.

3.2.2 Marketization of Urban Land Use

In March 1998, Ministry of Land and Resource (MLR) was founded to consolidate the former State Land Administration Bureau, Ministry of Geology and Mineral Resources, State Oceanic Administration Bureau and State Bureau of Surveying and Mapping. That symbolized efforts by the state to deal with the complex land use issues. In light of the pervasive cross-track land speculations by those quasi-governmental developers, the MLR issued the No. 11 Decree of Regulations on Granting LURs via Tender, Auction and Quotation in May 2002 that explicitly stipulated the LURs of all sites intended for commerce, tourism, entertainment activities and commodity-based housing projects must be granted through public processes of tender, auction or quotation instead of state assignment or private negotiation (MLR, 2002). In other words, the dual-track system in granting LURs would be replaced by a market-based one.

The No. 11 Decree, however, did not immediately generate the desired effects because of strong objections from the municipalities that had been granting LURs to developers at negotiated prices in order to attract inward investment. Many of them were afraid that implementation of No. 11 Decree would drive up urban land prices and discourage developers from investing. The city of Beijing, for example, tried to mitigate that impact by promulgating the municipal Circular on Regulations Regarding the Termination of Negotiated LURs Granting for Commercial Development before 1 July, the effective date of No. 11 Decree (Municipal Government of Beijing, 2002). It made exceptions to the No. 11 Decree by reserving negotiation as one of the legitimate pricing approaches for land uses in fields of greenbelt, small-town construction, urban renovation, and high-tech development.

Despite these municipal objections, No. 11 Decree did deter some of the negotiation-based land transactions. Nationwide, the number of cases where the LURs were granted via negotiation increased from 99,632 in 2000, through 145,228 in 2001, to 203,866 in 2002 but abruptly dropped to 157,381 in 2003. To completely end negotiation-based LURs granting for commercial developments, the MLR issued No. 71 Decree, Circular on Continuing the Supervision over Granting LURs for Commercial Development via Tender, Auction and Quotation in March 2004 (MLR, 2004), that explicitly set 31 August of that year as the deadline beyond which no exceptions could be made to the regulations as originally specified in the No. 11 Decree. That forced the municipal government of Beijing to issue the Supplementary Regulations on Terminating the Negotiated LURs Granting for Commercial Development in which the exemptions it once granted to land use projects in those four categories were annulled (Municipal Government of Beijing, 2004).

Note that those regulations on the primary land market still reserved state assignment or private negotiation as legitimate approaches to grant LURs for manufacturing production. The reason that manufacturing land uses were exempt from state decrees, as will be demonstrated in the next chapter, was to leave localities an effective tool to attract manufacturing investments, boost labor employment and expedite industrial development. Such a "back door," however, made it possible to transfer the LURs acquired via assignment or negotiation for manufacturing activities to prospective users in the secondary land market who were interested in commercial development. In order to prevent that speculation, the MLR updated the Directory of Allocated Land and substantially narrowed the scope of recipients eligible for free land assignment. For example, most corporatized or privatized former SOEs were excluded from the list. The number of free-of-charge land assignment cases shrank from 160,284 in 2000 to 30,747 in 2006 (MLR, 2007). Secondly, only SOEs could be authorized to transfer their LURs to commercial developers and it had to be approved by their supervising governmental organs and conducted via public tender, auction or quotation. Thirdly, the allocated land of SOEs could be used as capital investments in the newly founded corporatized enterprises when many SOEs were insolvent in the late 1990s. That was a cost-effective approach for local governments to rescue those firms from bankruptcy, which made the alternative to transfer the land to commercial developers a less appealing option. As a result of all these policies, most LURs for real estate development had to be priced through tender, auction and quotation on the open market. Driven by the explosive growth of housing demand since 1998, residential development has been the dominating domain of urban land use since 2003 with the second largest sector of commerce/service lagging far behind (see Table 3.3).

Table 3.3   LURs granted via tender, auction or quotation, 2003–2006

		Residence	Commerce/ service	Manufacturing/ storage	Public facilities	Transportation
2003	Cases (no.)	22,269	23,340	2,741	1,313	87
	Acreage (ha.)	25,654.32	19,466.14	4,683.77	3,903.85	83.82
2004	Cases (no.)	21,079	21,330	2,422	1,507	197
	Acreage (ha.)	27,524.21	19,079.67	4,440.21	869.8	152.22
2005	Cases (no.)	2,4223	17,094	2,381	525	13
	Acreage (ha.)	35,650.83	16,390.53	4,309.27	775.45	8.26
2006	Cases (no.)	26,008	16,892	2,229	550	18
	Acreage (ha.)	46,160.05	19,066.67	4,688.39	1,140.07	28.86

Source: *China Land and Resources Almanac*, 2004–2007.

3.3 Local Strategies to Expedite Urban Growth

The urban housing and land use reforms were originally intended by the central state to improve the housing provision and land use efficiencies by substituting market mechanisms for the state involvements in both systems. Motivated by the revenue prospects associated with urban real estate development, however, local states took advantage of the new housing and land use schemes to boost their own financial strength via an approach that was much less discernible than directly operating business as prevailed in the early 1990s (Duckett, 1998). Specifically, as the de facto owner of most urban land (except some land under the control of organizations administered by the central state such as army, central SOEs, universities, and so on), municipalities could drive the interrelated land and housing prices up by manipulating the acreages and the floor area ratios (FARs) of land used for real estate development, which may generate higher "land granting premium" and tax revenues that can used to launch large-scale urban construction projects and attract manufacturing investments.

3.3.1 Controlled Supply of Land for Real Estate Development

The supply and the FARs of land are commanded by the municipalities that would like to grant LURs to developers at higher prices. Since developers can no longer get the LURs through approaches other than tender, auction and quotation, limited supply in the primary land market would drive up the land price and motivate developers to build structures with higher FARs. More often than not, variance of FARs can be approved by planning departments with ease because the improved city height and sharper city image associated with higher FARs can make the urban land even more valuable, which has been deemed by many municipal officials as an important means of urban asset management (*cheng shi jing ying*).

In the meantime, urban land for real estate development was made even less available by those developers who, anticipating increasingly higher property price in the future, left the land they had LURs over idle without launching any development for months or years, a strategy called "land hoarding" (*tun di*). Those land stocks can be used either as collateral to get more bank loans or as valuable assets in support of the share price of those firms listed on the stock market, which in turn provide them additional capital to purchase land. As a result of governmental tactics and corporate strategies, urban land price indices soared in 2002 when the No. 11 Decree became effective nationwide and controlled land supply was able to generate a substantial effect on the land price (see Figure 3.1). It should be noted that residential land prices (both general and luxury), as denoted by the slopes of the corresponding lines in Figure 3.1, grew faster than the land prices for office and commercial development, which suggests the significance of residential land development to both real estate investors and the municipalities.

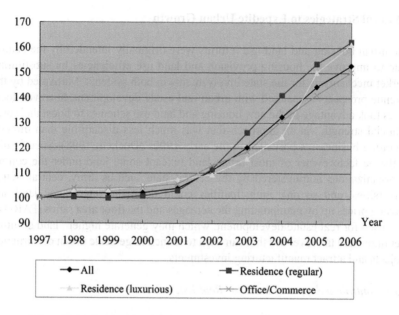

Figure 3.1   Index of national land price, 1997–2006

Note: Land price index in 1997 is set to be 100.

Source: *China Statistical Yearbook*, various years.

The rapidly rising urban land prices were immediately translated into rocketing housing costs on the market. The national average prices of regular residential units increased by 74 percent from 1,790 *yuan* per square meter in 1997 to 3,119 *yuan* per square meter in 2006 (see Table 3.4). Most of that price rise occurred after 2003, one year following the implementation of No. 11 Decree. Housing prices grew even faster in more developed regions. For example, the average housing price across 35 major cities including 27 capital cities of provinces and autonomous regions, 4 municipalities directly under the central government and four cities of Daliao, Qingdao, Ningbo and Xiamen, was still 2,267 *yuan* per square meter in 2002 but already reached 4,350 *yuan* per square meter in 2006, an annual growth rate of nearly 20 percent, much higher than that of urban household disposable incomes that increased from 7,703 *yuan* in 2002 to 11,759 *yuan* in 2006 at an annual rate of 10 percent (SSB, various years-a). On the other hand, in face of the considerable revenue prospects associated with land granting premium, many municipalities were simply reluctant to supply land for the affordable housing program whose LURs were to be assigned free of charge. As presented in Table 3.2, floor areas of affordable housing units had been in stagnation since 2000 while those for the other development purposes kept increasing. Consequently, the strategies of local states to drive up land price and their shrinking role in providing social housing improved the municipal revenues at the expense of housing affordability for regular urban households.

Table 3.4   Prices of urban real estate, 1997–2006 (in *yuan*/square meter)

	Overall	Residence (all)	Residence (luxurious)	Office	Commerce
1997	1,997	1,790	5,382	4,677	3,090
1998	2,063	1,854	4,596	5,552	3,170
1999	2,053	1,857	4,503	5,265	3,333
2000	2,112	1,948	4,288	4,751	3,260
2001	2,170	2,017	4,348	4,588	3,274
2002	2,250	2,092	4,154	4,336	3,489
2003	2,359	2,197	4,145	4,196	3,675
2004	2,778	2,608	5,576	5,744	3,884
2005	3,168	2,937	5,834	6,923	5,022
2006	3,367	3,119	6,585	8,053	5,247

Source: *China Statistical Yearbook*, various years.

In view of the surging housing prices and its adverse impacts on social stability, China's central government has been repeatedly issuing regulations since 2005 to increase the supply of land used for residential development. For example, the Circular on Effectively Stabilizing Housing Prices that was promulgated by the State Council on May 9, 2005, or what Chinese call "State Eight Measures" (*guo ba tiao*) explicitly required municipalities to increase the supply of land for residential development (State Council, 2005), which was reaffirmed by the Opinions about Adjusting Housing Supply Structure to Stabilize Housing Price or "State Six Measure" (*guo liu tiao*) on 24 May 2006 (State Council, 2006a).

The exclusive focuses of these policies on housing issues, however, left the supply of land used for commercial and office purposes and the regulations on their FARs less attended. The acreage of land used for commercial and office development has continued to decrease since 2003 (see Table 3.3) while the floor areas of those structures built on them have been constantly increasing (see Table 3.2). The consequence was rising FARs of commercial land development projects as visually represented by the growing heights of office towers and central business districts (CBDs) across many Chinese cities, which improved the overall urban land value through the ubiquitous spatial externalities within an urban setting and largely counteracted the effects of those state policies to stabilize land price for residential development. The price record of urban land transactions in the primary market was constantly refreshed at different cities across China, which attracted increasing amounts of capital into real estate sector whose fixed asset investments were nearly one fourth of the nationwide total. In Beijing, for example, more than half of the fixed asset investments have occurred in real estate since the start of this century (SSB, 2008a). The growth of the Chinese economy has been increasingly dependent on the prosperity of real estate.

3.3.2 Growing Land Granting Premium and Extensive Urban Construction

The immediate outcome of rising urban property price and inelastic housing demand is the extraordinary land-granting premium that was to be collected by municipal governments. In 1999, one year after marketization of housing provision started, the nationwide gross premium was only 51.4 billion *yuan*, or less than 10 percent of local budgetary revenues (see Table 3.5). It increased by more than 15 times and reached 807.8 billion *yuan* in just seven years. In 2007, the record of 913 billion *yuan* was equivalent to 38 percent of local budgetary revenues (SSB, various years-a). It should be noted what municipalities eventually received from granting LURs, or the net premium (the third row in Table 3.5), was approximately one third of the gross magnitudes (the second row in Table 3.5). The other two-thirds were usually used to compensate the dislocated people originally living or working on the redeveloped land and to convert the acquired land into conditions ready for development through "five connections and one leveling" (*wu tong yi ping*, or connecting roads, water, drainage, electricity, telecommunications and the leveling of sites).

Table 3.5   Gross premium and net premium of granting LURs, 1999–2006 (in billion *yuan*)

	1999	2000	2001	2002	2003	2004	2005	2006
Gross premium	51.4	59.6	129.6	241.7	542.1	641.2	588.4	807.8
Net premium	(17)	(20)	(43)	(80)	179.9	234	218.4	297.8
Local budgetary revenue	559.5	640.6	780.3	851.5	985.0	1,189.3	1,510.1	1,830.4

Note: The parenthesized net premiums for 1999 to 2002 are estimated on the basis that the net premium is approximately one-third of the gross total.
Source: *China Land and Resources Almanac*, 2000–2007.

As illustrated in Chapter 2, one of the most outstanding features of local state entrepreneurialism in China is the extravagant public spending on urban construction projects to demonstrate the performance achieved under the leadership of officials. The wide scope of that enterprise ranging from utilities delivery through transportation facilities to mega-projects suggests it has to be financed by means other than regular tax revenues or even fees. Table 3.6 shows that land granting premium was the third largest financial source for urban construction projects in 2004. Although the data for more recent years is unavailable, it is not impossible that land granting premium might take the place of the "local taxes" or even "domestic loans" in 2005 or thereafter as the second or most important financial support to urban construction because of its rapidly growing magnitude and the close distance between it and that of other two sources. Neither is it difficult to understand that urban construction projects across most Chinese city projects had been much fewer in number and smaller in scale before land granting premium emerged in the late 1990s as a result of reforms in housing and the land use system. By that time, governmental investments in urban construction was mainly financed by tax revenues and administrative fees, which was inadequate to lever substantial bank loans or private investments.

Table 3.6   Financing urban construction, 2001–2004 (in billion *yuan*)

	2001	2002	2003	2004
Domestic loans	74.2	94.0	136.9	148.0
Local tax revenues	59.5	70.9	90.5	111.2
Land granting premium	16.7	28.3	50.7	110.0
Self-raised funds	41.0	60.1	77.0	90.0
Administrative fees	20.2	30.1	37.1	42.7
Foreign investments	5.6	6.9	7.7	8.7
Central expenditures	9.0	7.6	7.7	5.3
Stock financing	0.1	0.7	0.03	0.3
Bonds	0.7	0.3	1.6	0.06
Others	25.6	30.5	33.0	26.1
Total	252.6	315.6	427.6	525.8

Source: Urban Construction Yearbook of China, various years.

Not only did a considerable portion of investment in urban construction come from land granting premium, a major portion of this municipal revenue was also used for urban construction. Note that the expenditures of land granting premium in a given year were actually financed by the revenues collected in the previous year. This is because the management system of land granting premium was characterized by "separating revenue from expenditure accounts." Specifically, all revenues of land granting premium must be deposited into one designated account while the expenditures including those compensations for resident dislocation and land preparation must be withdrawn from a separate one. For each year, the fund available for disbursement was allocated *ex ante* from the revenue account to the expenditure one according to the projected needs of that year and the premium collected in the previous one. That means the 110 billion *yuan* land granting premium used for urban construction in 2004 (see Table 3.6) was actually drawn from the 179.9 billion *yuan* net land granting premium collected in 2003 (see Table 3.5). In other words, two-thirds of the net land granting premium was spent on projects to modernize cities physically.

Chapter 4

Competition for Manufacturing Investments and the Demand for FDI

As mentioned in the last chapter, private negotiation between municipalities and prospective investors to determine prices of land used for manufacturing production was exempt from state regulations on granting LURs via public tender, auction and quotation. Because of the critical significance of manufacturing industries to local economic growth as well as to political prospects of local officials, land that is one of the indispensable inputs to manufacturing activities was usually offered by municipalities at exceedingly low rates to attract investors. This chapter will investigate those particular municipal hospitalities and demonstrate how the sharply contrasting land-pricing strategies for real estate development on the one hand and manufacturing investments on the other led to the preference for FDI over domestic investments.

4.1 Significance of Manufacturing

Despite tremendous tax revenues and land granting premium it generated, the real estate sector is a less reliable pillar of local economic and revenue growth than manufacturing for the following reasons. First of all, growth of the urban real estate market, as shown in the last chapter, was largely driven by soaring land and housing prices that were increasingly too expensive for regular urban households. Their shrinking purchase power as relative to constantly rising urban housing prices posed a potential threat to sustained growth of tax revenues collected from the real estate sector because most of these taxes are levied on dynamic real estate transactions on the market rather than static property values. Property tax that has been present in many developed countries is still absent in China. In other words, tax revenues contributed by real estate sector may shrink if fewer transactions occur as a result of the price bubble. Secondly, land granting premium is a kind of one-off revenue for municipal governments because LURs are granted to residential developers for a period of 50 years and other developers for 70 years on a renewable basis (State Council, 1990b). Since the urban land is an increasingly scarce resource, the rapid urban real estate development means the land granting premium that can be generated in the future is being quickly depleted.

In contrast, manufacturing industries, without being subject to the vicissitudes of real estate market situation and the one-off nature of land granting premium, would be able to contribute more smooth tax revenues on the land where they operate. For example, VAT, the tax levied on added value regardless of profits, will be generated as soon as production processes start. Thus, the imperatives arising from a re-centralized fiscal system to mobilize revenue collection strongly motivated local states to compete for inward manufacturing investments. As a result, manufacturing has been the sector with largest contribution to local tax revenues even though the VAT it generates has to be shared with the central government and local tax revenues collected from real estate was less than 70 percent of those from manufacturing in 2006 (see Table 2.2). Accordingly, VAT has been the single tax category with greatest contribution to national total tax revenues (MOF, various years).

4.2 Land-Based Strategies to Attract Manufacturing Investments

Like building urban infrastructure to facilitate logistics and improve amenities, land price manipulation is another powerful tool widely and legitimately used by municipalities to attract investors because the costs of labor and capital and soft institutions such as local culture are not amenable to purposeful government actions in the short-term. The excessively low prices of land, however, would make it increasingly costly for the municipalities to host manufacturing projects when the overall urban land value was quickly raised and land resource constraint became tight. It is in this context that prospective projects would be screened on the basis of their efficiencies in land use so that the municipal revenues generated by manufacturing production could be maximized.

4.2.1 Pricing of Land for Manufacturing Production

According to the No. 11 and No. 71 Decrees, LURs must be publicly granted via tender, auction and quotation for all commercial development projects as well as for other circumstances where there are two or more competing users regardless of the particular use of the land. The competitive land use request by manufacturing investors, however, would rarely occur in practice. First of all, as most manufacturing land was planned on spacious urban peripheries, the probability of competing uses would be much lower than that in the commercial land use cases because the latter was usually located in compact urban cores. Secondly, since the state decrees did not explicitly require manufacturing LURs be granted via public tender, auction or quotation, prospective investors usually communicated with municipalities on a one-to-one basis as to the land area they were interested in. Even if conflicting land use requests arose, there would still be enough room for municipalities to coordinate before this information was released to the general public. As a result, the non-competing manufacturing land uses then made negotiation a legitimate approach that was most commonly used to grant LURs to investors. During the four years from 2003 to 2006, the number of cases where the LURs were granted to a manufacturing investor was 214,888 and the total acreage was 429,947.4 hectares, among which 95 percent, or 203,607 cases with the acreage of 406,064.8 hectares were conducted through private negotiations (see Table 4.1).

Table 4.1   Granting LURs to manufacturing investors, 2003–2006

		2003	2004	2005	2006	Total
Negotiation	Cases (no.)	56,086	48,900	40,646	57,975	203,607
	Acreage (ha.)	94,751.2	85,347.9	86,202.5	139,763.2	406,064.8
	Price ($yuan$/m²)	113.7	119.2	129.9	117	–
Tender, auction & quotation	Cases (no.)	2,741	2,422	2,381	2,229	9,773
	Acreage (ha.)	4,683.8	4,440.2	4,309.3	4,688.4	18,121.7
	Price ($yuan$/m²)	363.2	376.4	303.4	185.8	–
Assignment	Cases (no.)	4,537	4,254	2,415	1,255	12,461
	Acreage (ha.)	7,067.1	10,345.5	10,537.7	5,760.9	33,711.2
	Price ($yuan$/m²)	–	–	–	–	–

Source: *China Land and Resources Almanac*, 2004–2006.

The consequence of ubiquitous use of negotiation was that prices of land used for manufacturing production were set astonishingly lower than they were supposed to be, which could be reflected by the following two observations. First of all, most but not all LURs for manufacturing production were granted through negotiations. Some were conducted via public tender, auction and quotation. The negotiated land prices for manufacturing production, however, were much lower than those for the same type of land use but determined on the market basis. For example, the negotiation-based manufacturing land prices were 113.7, 119.2 and 129.9 *yuan* per square meter for the three years from 2003 to 2005 respectively, while the those determined through tender, auction and quotation were as high as 363.2, 376.4, 303.4 *yuan* per square meter (see Table 4.1).

Secondly, prices of land for manufacturing activities did not demonstrate a significant rise even when the overall urban land value was rapidly growing. The price index of urban land for manufacturing production, for example, had been quite stable since the late 1990s. It increased by only 15 percent over the 9-year period from 1997 to 2006, with an average annual growth rate of mere 1.5 percent (SSB, various years-a) which was much lower than that of price indices of land used for residential or commercial development as graphed in Figure 3.1. The latter rose at an annual rate of 4.5 percent and increased by at least 50 percent during that same period of time. Detailed data on land prices across 35 major cities also present the divergence between land prices for manufacturing and those for residential or commercial development.[1] From 2000 to 2007, average land prices for manufacturing production slightly increased from 444 to 507 *yuan* per square meter while the residential and commercial land prices jumped from 923 to 1,702 *yuan* per square meter and from 1,615 to 2,509 *yuan* per square meter respectively (see Figure 4.1).

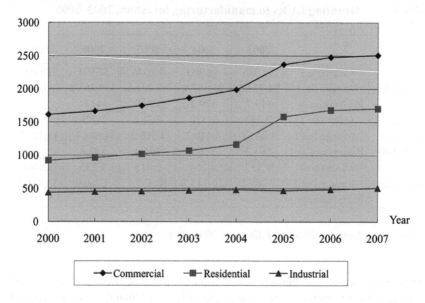

Figure 4.1   Average land prices across 35 major Chinese cities, 2000–2007 (in *yuan*/square meter)

Source: http://www.landvalue.com.cn/.

The absence of significant manufacturing land price growth could hardly be interpreted as an outcome resulting from pure market forces. Rather, it was the consequence of state intervention that could be clearly reflected by the gap between negotiated land prices and those determined through tender, auction and quotation. An additional piece of evidence for that state action was relatively heavier expenditure by municipalities on manufacturing land in order to convert it into the conditions that are most appealing to prospective investors than that

---

1   The 35 cities include the four municipalities of Beijing, Tianjin, Shanghai and Chongqing as well as Shijiazhuang, Nanjing, Hangzhou, Ningbo, Fuzhou, Xiamen, Jinan, Qingdao, Guangzhou, Shenzhen, Haikou in the east, Taiyuan, Hefei, Nanchang, Zhengzhou, Wuhan, Changsha in the middle, Huhehaote, Nanning, Chengdu, Guiyang, Kunming, Xian, Lanzhou, Xining, Yinchuan, Wulumuqi in the west and Shenyang, Dalian, Changchun, Harbin in the northeast

spent on land used for residential or commercial development. For example, land for manufacturing production was usually well served by municipalities with "seven connections and one leveling" (*qi tong yi ping*, connecting gas, heat in addition to the ordinary five connections of roads, water, drainage, electricity, telecommunications and the leveling of sites) or even "nine connections and one leveling" (*jiu tong yi ping*, connecting cable TV and broadband internet in addition to the seven items above). It has been shown in the last chapter that local states could only receive a portion, approximately one-third of the gross land granting premium at the end with the rest spent on compensating dislocated urban residents or rural farmers and consolidating land for development. Then a lower ratio of net land granting premium to the gross means more intensive efforts made by municipalities in land consolidation or preparation as presented in Table 4.2; the ratio of net to gross land granting premium for manufacturing land has been lower than one-third for years while those for residential or commercial development are consistently higher than that critical level.

Table 4.2   Premium of industrial, residential and commercial LURs granting, 2003–2006 (premium in billion *yuan*)

		2003	2004	2005	2006
Manufacturing	Gross premium	124.7	118.4	125	172.2
	Net premium	33.4	36.9	39.1	50.2
	Net/gross	**0.268**	0.312	0.313	0.292
Residential	Gross premium	259	326	296.9	452.9
	Net premium	82.5	120	114.3	177.6
	Net/gross	0.319	0.368	0.385	0.392
Commercial	Gross premium	138.6	182	147.4	167.2
	Net premium	57.8	72.8	57.2	64.6
	Net/gross	0.417	0.400	0.388	0.386

Source: *China Land and Resources Almanac*, 2004–2007.

4.2.2 Implications for Land Use Efficiencies

The municipal demand for manufacturing investments mirrored by the manipulation of land prices is not a recent phenomenon which was observed only in this century as the presented data indicates. It occurred in the early 1990s before the "tax assignment system" was implemented. As mentioned in Chapter 2, localities were strongly motivated to raise their revenues in 1993 because the central government would fill any gap, if any, between local budgetary revenues of that year and those collected under the new fiscal scheme. Then greater local revenue achievements in 1993 meant less impact of the "tax assignment system" on their revenue prospects for 1994, the consequence of which was extensive establishment of development zones and soaring FDI inflows in the mid 1990s.

The absence of well-institutionalized urban land market in the 1990s, however, failed to generate incentives for local states that are the de facto owner of most urban land to seek substantial returns to their supply of land used for manufacturing production. As elaborated in the last chapter, land use had been free in urban China until 1987 when the first case of granting LURs occurred in Shenzhen. The "land use regulation" that was promulgated in 1990 did not end the extensive involvement of state in the provision of land for commercial or residential development either. The resulting low prices of land used for those purposes also suggested low direct costs of compensating those original residents displaced by land acquisition as well as low opportunity costs associated with granting LURs to manufacturing investors. Thus, municipal demand for returns to their land provision would be weak, and large tracts of land were occupied by such manufacturing firms as those capitalized by the low-profile round-tripping FDI that were characterized by extensive use of land in an inefficient way.

The institutionalization of urban land markets at the beginning of the twenty-first century, especially market-based land pricing through public tender, auction and quotation, quickly raised the prices of land that was used for commercial or residential development. On the other hand, LURs for manufacturing production has been granted through private negotiation at excessively low rates. Under some circumstances, they were even generously offered by municipalities to manufacturing investors free of charge in exchange of their investment commitments (NAO, 2008). The widening gap between these two prices meant that alternative uses of land for residential or commercial development would generate much greater land granting premium which municipalities could collect. It also suggested higher displacement costs associated with acquiring land from its original urban residents or rural farmers. Given these, the motivation of granting LURs to manufacturing investors at preferential rates was not based on considerations of immediate benefits associated with property development. Rather, it was to build a manufacturing sector as a more reliable engine of local economic and revenue growth than a real estate sector could be. The success of this trade-off strategy then depends on the performance of the prospective manufacturing firm.

Because the combination of land and capital either in the form of real estate development or manufacturing production may generate tremendous municipal revenues and promote local economic growth, many acres of arable land were forcibly acquired by municipalities and then converted into those more profitable uses without just compensation to farmers originally occupying it. As presented in Table 4.3, the total acreage of arable land shrank from 129.2 million hectares to 121.8 million hectares between 1999 and 2006 with a substantial portion of the disappearing 7.4 million hectares used for real estate development or manufacturing activities. In 2006, the acreage of reclaimed land used for these two purposes reached the new records of 14,244 and 64,899 hectares respectively (MLR, various years). Even the highest compensation to farmers determined according to the standard of 30 times of the annual agricultural output value produced on the land they had been cultivating for generations was still inadequate to support their new lives without land, formal employment or social security.[2] In fact, the compensation which most displaced farmers received was usually much less than those maximum figures, and even nil in some extreme cases, which caused serious social opposition and even escalated into violent collisions between the deprived farmers and local states in many places (CCTV, 2008).

Table 4.3   Nationwide land acreage, 1999–2006 (in million ha.)

	1999	2000	2001	2002	2003	2004	2005	2006
Arable land	129.2	128.2	127.6	125.9	123.4	122.4	122.1	121.8
Park land	10.0	10.6	10.6	10.8	11.1	11.3	11.6	11.8
Woodland	228.3	228.8	229.2	230.7	234.0	235.1	235.7	236.1
Grassland	264.4	263.8	263.9	263.5	263.1	262.7	262.1	261.9
Developed land	24.6	24.7	24.9	25.7	25.4	25.7	26.0	26.4
Transportation land	5.7	5.8	5.8	2.1	2.2	2.2	2.3	2.4

Source: *China Land and Resources Almanac*, 2000–2007.

Threats that relentless land acquisition posed to crop production and social stability prompted the Chinese central state to curb those ambitious actions of local states by raising the standard of compensation to dislocated farmers and centralizing local land use plans. For example, the MLR issued the Guidelines on Improving the Compensation and Settlement associated with Land Acquisition in November 2004 to explicitly specify the new standards of compensation (MLR, 2004). Land granting premium was also permitted for the first time to be used as a complementary aid if the lives of displaced farmers could not be maintained as high as their original levels even according to the highest compensation standard. Moreover, the 11th Five-year Plan for the Development of National Economic and Social Development (2006–2011) explicitly set 120 million hectares in 2006 as the bottom line of arable land acreage that must be secured against aggressive acquisitions (State Council, 2006b). In order to ensure the national total acreages of arable land can be safely maintained above that line, it was also stipulated that land use plans of local governments on all levels had to be examined and approved by the central state.

The fact that land has become an increasingly tight physical constraint for urban development and costs of land acquisitions are significantly rising has encouraged municipalities to promote more intensive use of land resource by

---

2   See Article 47 of the Land Administration Law of PRC amended in 2004.

screening prospective firms in this regard. When an infinite and cheap supply of land for real estate development and manufacturing production could hardly be sustained, a more intensive land use pattern had to take the place of the extensive land use pattern that prevailed in the early 1990s so that economic outputs could be maximized on given land areas. Specifically, the acreage of land municipal governments offered to individual manufacturing projects was generally commensurate with the magnitude of investment in order to improve land use intensity. Intensity as measured in terms of input, however, does not necessarily guarantee efficiency on the side of output. Even prospective projects operating in the same sector with equivalent investment may end up in distinct outcomes due to their different marketing, management or technological abilities. Unfortunately, the asymmetric information between prospective investors and host municipalities usually made it very difficult or costly for the latter to gain in-depth knowledge of those critical qualitative natures. In most cases, their prospects of success always looked and sounded sanguine from documents prepared and words voiced by investors who were looking for preferential treatments offered by municipalities. The strategy widely used by municipalities was to assign heavier weight to those projects with foreign control, which was not only more visible but was also deemed on the basis of common experiences as the symbol of greater probability of success. The pecking order of prospective firms, with *Fortunes 500* multi-nations on the top, regular FIEs in the middle and domestic ones at the bottom was extensively practiced across municipalities in China.

4.3 Ownership-Specific Advantages of Manufacturing FIEs

The impressions of most municipalities that FIEs had superior land use efficiencies which resulted in municipal preference toward them were not unfounded. On an aggregate basis, the daily operations of manufacturing FIEs in China proved to be more efficient in terms of tax revenues as well as other tangible economic achievements such as GDP generated on unit acreage of land. Furthermore, their advantages in land use efficiency on the plant level were translated through the localization strategies adopted by many FIEs into stronger linkage effects that might give rise to the hub-and-spoke clustering type as identified by Markusen (1996). Thus, hosting FIEs capitalized by real FDI was a more cost-effective approach to promoting local economic growth than attracting individual investors on a case-by-case basis. We now turn to the individual and collective advantages of FIEs as the final part of the big story that gave rise to the FDI dynamics as identified at the beginning of this book.

4.3.1 Plant-Level Advantages

This book uses fixed assets as a proxy of land area occupied by manufacturing firms because information on the latter is unavailable and the acreage of land provided to manufacturing investors was usually set by the hosting municipalities to be commensurate with the size of their investments. Thus, the ratios of VAT/EIT/output to fixed assets as presented in Table 4.4 approximately measured land use efficiencies of FIEs and domestic firms. Manufacturing projects capitalized by FDI demonstrated higher efficiencies of land use than domestic firms. Both the ratios of VAT to fixed assets and the ratios of EIT to fixed assets for FIEs have consistently been higher than those of domestic firms since 2000, even though most FIEs were subject to the preferential EIT rate of 15 percent that was less than half of the regular rate of 33 percent for Chinese domestic firms. That suggested manufacturing FIEs generated more tax revenues than domestic peers with given amount of fixed assets, or land inputs.

In addition, manufacturing FIEs also produced greater value of output on unit acreage of land than domestic firms did, which meant their greater contributions to local GDP growth as well as the political prospects of local leadership with a given amount of land provision. Although the figures of fixed assets as presented in Table 4.4 only stood for those firms above a designated size (*gui mo yi shang*) with annual revenues of over 5 million *yuan* earned from principal businesses in the manufacturing sector, the results may be generalized for all firms as long as it is reasonably assumed the total fixed assets of domestic firms below a designated

Table 4.4   Fixed assets and tax contributions of domestic manufacturing firms and FIEs, 2000–2006 (fixed assets in billion *yuan*)

		Fixed assets (FA)	$\dfrac{\text{VAT}}{\text{FA}}$ (%)	$\dfrac{\text{EIT}}{\text{FA}}$ (%)	$\dfrac{\text{Output}}{\text{FA}}$ (%)
2000	FIEs	830.8	8.8	1.7	272.8
	Domestic firms	2,617.5	6.4	0.8	200.4
2001	FIEs	920.1	10.7	2.0	282.8
	Domestic firms	2,687.7	7.5	1.4	217.3
2002	FIEs	1,002.9	12.6	2.0	341.0
	Domestic firms	2,818.6	8.4	1.1	224.4
2003	FIEs	1,153.4	13.1	2.2	402.6
	Domestic firms	3,016.2	9.6	1.2	252.7
2004	FIEs	1,583.3	11.1	2.1	402.1
	Domestic firms	3,412.7	10.2	1.5	327.1
2005	FIEs	1,830.7	11.8	2.0	420.9
	Domestic firms	3,871.4	10.4	1.8	363.6
2006	FIEs	2,239.7	12.4	2.1	433.3
	Domestic firms	4,454.1	10.3	2.4	398.5

Source: *China Industry Economy Statistical Yearbook* and *Tax Yearbook of China*, various years.

size (*gui mo yi xia*) with annual revenues less than 5 million *yuan* earned from principal businesses were much more than those of corresponding FIEs. In that case, the gap between the ratio of taxes to the fixed assets of all domestic firms and that ratio for all FIEs would be even wider.

Detailed statistics on the sub-sectoral basis shows that manufacturing FIEs had higher land use efficiencies than their domestic peers in most technology- or capital-intensive manufacturing industries. Table 4.5 presents the ratios of VAT to fixed assets for FIEs and domestic firms respectively across 14 major manufacturing industries that had complete data records. Manufacturing FIEs demonstrated higher ratios of VAT to fixed assets in those industries highlighted in bold that were typically characterized by intensive input of capital, technology, or both. For example, machinery and equipment industries need substantial investment. Technological sophistication is indispensable from chemical and medical product manufacturing. Business success in the sector of beverage and food requires a great deal of R&D on the recipes and demands considerable expense on advertising and marketing. Although the ratios of domestic firms in the other manufacturing sub-sectors were literally higher than those of FIEs, the gaps are neither significant in magnitude nor consistent over time.

Table 4.5   Ratios of VAT to fixed assets for major manufacturing sub-sectors, 2004–2006 (%)

	2004		2005		2006	
	FIEs	**DFs**	**FIEs**	**DFs**	**FIEs**	**DFs**
Tobacco	25.5	50.2	17.1	51.3	11.7	57.4
Beverage	12.0	6.7	13.6	6.8	14.8	7.5
Food manufacturing	9.7	3.9	12.0	4.2	12.9	4.3
Petroleum processing	7.1	11.1	8.9	10.2	8.5	9.0
Chemical products	11.1	8.2	9.6	8.7	9.3	7.7
Medical products	13.9	8.2	15.4	8.0	16.0	7.8
Rubber products	6.7	7.9	8.0	8.7	8.3	8.1
Nonmetallic mineral products	5.5	5.8	5.8	5.6	6.4	6.2
Ferrous metal smelting	12.2	9.7	12.9	10.1	12.5	9.1
Nonferrous metal smelting	5.5	7.6	9.3	9.2	14.0	11.2
Specific-purpose machinery	8.4	5.5	10.1	7.4	12.7	8.8
Transportation equipment	14.7	9.1	14.9	7.9	14.2	8.2
Electric machinery	12.5	10.2	12.1	10.5	15.4	11.6
Telecommunication equipments	6.5	9.8	6.1	9.9	9.1	12.3

Note: "DFs" denote domestic firms.

Source: *China Industry Economy Statistical Yearbook*, 2006 and 2007.

The only two exceptions were tobacco and telecommunication where the ratios of FIEs had been lower than those of their domestic peers. It should be noted, however, that entry of FDI in the tobacco industry had been under the strict restriction of the Guiding Catalogue on Industries for Foreign Investment (NDRC and MOC, 2007). In 2007, there was only six FIEs nationwide in this particular industry with fixed assets of 0.66 billion *yuan* as opposed to 144 domestic ones with total fixed assets of 66.4 billion *yuan* (SSB, various years-b), which made the VAT-to-fixed asset ratio of FIEs a much less accurate indicator of their land use efficiencies than it was in other industries. On the other hand, deeper investigation in the industry of telecommunication suggests tax revenue was not the only motivation driving the municipal hunger for manufacturing FIEs. Stronger stimulating effects to the overall local economies generated by FIEs than by domestic firms could well maintain municipal preference for them even if they contributed less tax revenue than domestic peers did on their own (Sun, 2008). As opposed to the few FDI in the tobacco industry, there were 4,965 FIEs in telecommunication sector out of 60,016 FIEs across all 30 manufacturing industries. The fixed assets of those 4,965 FIEs were 385.7 billion *yuan* that amounted to be 17 percent of the fixed assets of all manufacturing FIEs.

The weaker ability of telecommunication FIEs to generate tax revenue as reflected by their significantly lower VAT-to-fixed asset ratios contrasted sharply with the extraordinary value of output they produced. Statistics show the aggregate outputs associated with FIEs and their domestic peers of that particular sector in 2006 were 2,717.2 and 590.5 billion *yuan* respectively and their corresponding output-to-fixed asset ratios were 7.0 and 5.5 (SSB, various years-b). Because the magnitude of added value is approximately the difference between output value and intermediate inputs of tangible materials, lower added value and higher output of FIEs in the telecommunication industry meant they might use much more intermediate inputs than their domestic peers did. A full investigation of the causes is beyond the scope of this book. A plausible explanation was that FIEs in the telecommunication industry substituted intensive intermediate inputs such as machinery for extensive use of labor. The implication of their heavier use of intermediate inputs was that telecommunication FIEs made greater contributions to local GDP growth through the industrial linkage effects as will be elaborated below than domestic ones did, even though that was achieved at the expense of immediate VAT revenues. In other words, tax is not the only concern of municipalities hosting inward manufacturing investment. Equal importance was attached to the extent to which the prospective projects got involved in local industrial development.

Among manufacturing FIEs that are generally preferred by localities to domestic firms, those with substantial magnitudes of investments may receive even better treatments and gain increasing popularities. Due to their focus on the economic benefits associated with inward manufacturing investments, municipalities are highly concerned with the prospects of manufacturing project. Magnitude of investment is usually deemed as an important indicator of the strength of investors and the probability of their business success. As presented by Table 4.6, large- and medium-sized manufacturing firms (denoted by "L&M") were less liable to be in deficit than the small-sized ones (denoted by "S"), which was particularly true for the industry of telecommunication equipment that FIEs overwhelmingly dominated. In 2006, more than 80 percent of the industrial output in telecommunication was produced by FIEs, as opposed to only more than 40 percent in transportation equipment and electrical machinery industries. The average performance of manufacturing FIEs with different sizes convinced many Chinese officials of the superiorities of projects with greater investment and larger capacity of production. That gave rise to the growth ideology of "doing big and doing strong" (*zuo da zu qiang*) in their minds as well as ascending "size index" of FDI as identified in the first chapter.

Table 4.6   Proportions of deficit manufacturing firms, 2003–2006 (%)

		2003	2004	2005	2006
Telecommunication equipments	L&M	15.1	18.8	18.2	16.1
	S	24.7	28.5	25.2	22.2
Transportation equipments	L&M	17.0	17.7	17.6	13.4
	S	19.6	21.8	18.8	16.9
Electric machinery	L&M	14.2	14.8	14.0	12.2
	S	17.6	14.8	16.8	14.7
All manufacturing sectors	L&M	15.9	17.1	16.3	14.3
	S	18.5	21.1	17.5	15.3

Source: China Industry Economy Statistical Yearbook, various years.

4.3.2 Industrial Linkage Effects

In addition to their advantages on the plant level, FIEs were also characterized by their stronger industrial linkage effects and heavier use of intermediate inputs. One example was FIEs in the telecommunication industry as demonstrated before. For most municipalities, the policy implication of such production pattern associated with FIEs was to build a cluster of supplying firms around them, which could be a more effective approach to expedite local economic growth than hosting individual firms that had looser or no local connections to one another.

4.3.2.1 Conceptual issues
Linkage effect refers to the inter-sectoral input–output relations within an economy (Leontief, 1941; Rasmussen, 1956; Hirschman, 1958; Chenery and Clark, 1959; Leontief, 1966). Input involves material intermediate products such as machinery, raw materials, semi-finished products for further processing and parts for final

assembly, all of which will be transformed via production process into output commodities. It should be noted that labor and land are not deemed as intermediate inputs in industrial linkage analysis because they are not the products of any particular industry and do not have impact on the inter-sectoral relations. Input–output linkages can be divided into two categories, namely backward linkage and forward linkage. The former measures the demand derived from incremental production of a given sector for inputs produced by its upstream industries. It occurs when the growth of one sector leads to the growth of industries that supply it. The forward linkage, in the other way, refers to the product supply of a given sector to its downstream sectors. It represents the response of other domestic manufacturers to the production of their intermediate inputs by a given sector.

More often than not, backward linkage effects are more important in linkage analysis and industrial planning. This is because backward linkage focuses the demand-side stimulus generated by a sector to the whole economy. Compared to forward linkage that deals with supply-side potential impact on the downstream industries, backward linkage is a more feasible tool for policy makers to identify key industries whose growth will promote the development of a wide range of sectors through demand-side imperatives rather than supply-side possibilities. In general, manufacturing industries have higher backward linkage effects than primary industries that mainly depend on natural endowments instead of produced commodities as their inputs. Among manufacturing industries, sectors that make products with higher added value such as telecommunication equipment are expected to have higher backward linkage effects than those producing low-value-added products like mining. Note this statement does not contradict previous discussion about low added value of FIEs in the telecommunication industry because that comparison is between domestic firms and FIEs but here it is between telecommunication and other manufacturing industries. Given the significance of manufacturing industries to the Chinese local economy as addressed in the last chapter, local policy makers usually target sectors that have high backward linkage effects as "pillar industries" to host inward investment.

4.3.2.2 Backward linkage effects of FIEs

The backward linkage index is also named as its multiplier coefficient because an increase in final demand that includes private or government consumption, fixed asset formation and exports may pass its effects backward through all related upstream industries and lead to the increase of overall output by a multiplier. Hence, a large multiplier coefficient means a stronger linkage effect and a low multiplier coefficient suggests a weaker linkage effect. Computed on the basis of the latest China 2002 Input–output Table (SSB, 2003a), Table 4.7 presents 10 major manufacturing sub-sectors with the largest multiplier coefficients in 2001.

In order to evaluate the backward linkage effects of FIEs as opposed to Chinese domestic firms, it is necessary to investigate both their magnitudes of intermediate inputs and their correlations with the multiplier coefficients of each individual sector. Because multiplier effect as a consequence is triggered by input–

output nature of production, the correlation coefficients between input magnitudes of different firm groups and multiplier coefficients reflect the strength of their causal relationship. On the other hand, the aggregate magnitude of intermediate inputs may shed light on the potential impacts of the linkage effects on local economies. For example, suppose FIEs and domestic firms have close magnitudes of intermediate inputs but the correlation coefficient of the former is significantly higher than that of the latter. That means the observed pattern of industrial linkages should be mainly attributed to the production activities of FIEs. Alternatively, if they have equivalent correlation coefficients but FIEs use greater magnitudes of intermediate inputs, it suggests FIEs may have a bigger impact on local economic growth than domestic firms do.

Table 4.7   Multiplier coefficients and intermediate inputs of manufacturing sectors, 2002

	Multiplier coefficients	Intermediate inputs (in billion *yuan*)		
		FIEs	SOEs	Collective firms
Apparel	3.09	98.0	8.6	15.2
Leather, fur products	3.20	71.5	4.0	6.6
Chemical Fibers	3.17	22.4	30.3	3.8
Plastics	3.18	76.0	15.3	15.4
Nonferrous metal smelting	3.13	26.8	85.2	17.3
Metal products	3.14	88.9	22.8	22.4
Transportation equipments	3.17	191.8	394.7	24.3
Electric machinery	3.21	150.0	68.8	47.4
Telecommunication equipments	3.54	655.0	219.9	4.3
Measuring instruments	3.26	52.9	13.0	2.3
Intermediate inputs	–	2,280.4	2,461.7	420.3
Correlation coefficients	–	0.46	0.08	0.22

Note: Intermediate inputs and correlation coefficient are for all manufacturing sub-sectors.

Source: China 2002 Input–Output Table; *China Industry Economy Statistical Yearbook*, various years.

As shown in Table 4.7, the correlation coefficients of manufacturing FIEs, SOEs and collective firms were 0.46, 0.08 and 0.22 respectively. The aggregate intermediate inputs used by all manufacturing FIEs amounted to 2,280.4 billion *yuan* in 2002, close to those of SOEs but much greater than those of collective firms. Assuming production technology or the input–output interdependence has not experienced significant change since 2002 and the multiplier coefficients as presented in Table 4.7 can be applied to subsequent years of 2003, 2005 and

2006, examination of the correlation coefficients also generates similar results (see Table 4.8). In 2003, for example, the correlation coefficients for FIEs, SOEs and collective firms were 0.40, 0.16 and 0.29 with their respective uses of intermediate inputs of 3,275.82, 3,457.03, and 690.68 billion *yuan*. Although correlation coefficient for private firms that are deemed as the most dynamic element of Chinese economy reached 0.31 in 2005, next only to that of FIEs, their intermediate inputs of 3,383.7 billion *yuan* lagged far behind the 5,939.2 billion *yuan* as achieved by FIEs. In 2006, the gap between correlation coefficients of these groups remained intact but that between intermediate inputs became even wider.

Table 4.8   Correlation   coefficients   and   intermediate   inputs   of manufacturing FIEs, SOEs, private firms and collective firms, 2002–2006 (intermediate inputs in billion *yuan*)

		FIEs	SOEs	Private firms	Collective firms
2002	Coefficient	0.46	0.08	–	0.22
	Inputs	2,280.4	2,461.7	–	420.3
2003	Coefficient	0.40	0.16	–	0.29
	Inputs	3,198.6	2,934.6	–	639.9
2005	Coefficient	0.40	0.11	0.31	0.26
	Inputs	5,799.1	4,150.6	3,383.7	547.2
2006	Coefficient	0.41	0.10	0.32	0.28
	Inputs	7,300.0	4,779.2	4,680.4	578.7

Note: Intermediate inputs computed as the difference between industrial outputs and value added.

Source: China 2002 Input–Output Table; *China Industry Economy Statistical Yearbook*, various years.

4.3.2.3 Domestic content of inputs

In an open economy, not all intermediate inputs is produced domestically. In the extreme case, if all intermediate inputs used by manufacturing FIEs in a host economy is imported from overseas, those firms do not have any backward linkage at all with suppliers within that country, even though they demonstrate considerable magnitude of intermediate inputs and the sectoral distribution of its intermediate inputs remains highly correlated with the multiplier coefficients. The concern of policy makers with the impact of industrial linkages on economic growth within their jurisdictions entails close examination of the *domestic content of inputs* because production domestic supplies can be localized with ease while it would be quite difficult to create local substitutions for supplies produced oversea.

The term "domestic" means geographical location within the national border rather than the non-foreign ownership of a firm. Thus, a domestic supplier could be an FIE. As the ratio of domestically produced supplies to the total intermediate inputs, domestic content of inputs for some industry can be calculated if its imported inputs are known. Unfortunately, the foreign trade statistics of China are organized according to the categories of goods, rather than their purposes either as intermediate inputs or as final demand. It is then unclear how much of the intermediate inputs used by FIEs and domestic firms are imported from abroad. Besides, not all of the imports are used as intermediate inputs. Many imported goods, especially those by FIEs, are simply resold to other firms. The available data of imports then sheds little light on how many go into the production process as intermediate inputs.

Despite the paucity of direct information on imported inputs or imports used as inputs, domestic content of inputs for manufacturing sectors can still be estimated on an inferential basis. It is noted that telecommunication equipments and transportation equipments are the two sectors with the highest magnitudes of intermediate inputs (see Table 4.7) and two of those with highly sophisticated production technology. If their domestic content of inputs can be identified, it is then reasonable to assume other sectors that demand less advanced technology have generally higher domestic content of inputs because it would make no sense for firms in those other sectors to transport a higher proportion of their physical supplies from abroad. For example, Volkswagen or Motorola may choose to import motor engines or microchips in order to prevent their competitors in China from learning the technological know-how. But Coca-Cola would not ship bottled liquids from overseas to China because local production of glass bottles would make their products more competitive on the market of China without any adverse impacts on their technological advantages over domestic rivals.

In the telecommunication industry, a significant and increasing share of intermediate inputs is produced by suppliers operating in China. Perhaps the most illuminating case in this regard is Motorola (China) Electronics Ltd., the largest telecommunication equipment FIE in China in 2005. Since its entry into China in 1992, Motorola has been rapidly improving its domestic content of inputs. In 1996, it purchased intermediate inputs of 260 million US$ from more than 130 suppliers within China. In the next couple of years, the value of domestically supplied inputs more than tripled reaching 550 million US$ in 1999 and 868 million in 2000. It had 700 Chinese domestic suppliers in 2001. As a result, the domestic content of inputs increased continuously from 35 percent in 1995, through 50 percent in 1996, 55 percent in 1997, 60 percent in 1998 to 65 percent in 2002 (Chen, 2003).

Following Motorola, more and more FIEs in telecommunication industry started to localize their supplies of inputs. Nanjing Ericsson, a joint venture between Swedish Ericsson and China Panda Group, not only kept increasing their purchases of domestic intermediate inputs, they also brought more than 70 of their global suppliers to China that were designated as one of their four global supplying bases. The domestic content of inputs of telephone exchanges and wireless base stations rocketed from nil and 5 percent in 1999 to 60 and 51 percent in 2001 respectively (Chen, 2001). Some of their mobile phone models such as T18 and A1018 had domestic content of over 60 percent with the battery and charger produced entirely in China. Tianjin Samsung Communication Technology Co. Ltd., a branch of Samsung China that specialized in the production of mobile communication terminals, as well as Beijing Nokia, the largest exporter of mobile telecommunication equipments in China, also set 65 and 60 percent as their respective targeted domestic content of inputs.

The localization strategy of production can also be observed in automobile industry, a key sub-sector within transportation equipment manufacturing. As the ground-breaker in localizing the production of auto parts, Shanghai Volkswagen today has one of the highest domestic content of inputs. With the strong support of Shanghai municipal government (Thun, 1999; Huang, 2003; Yu, 2005), the domestic content ratio of Santana, the model of a long history in China, has been constantly increasing from almost nil in 1983 when the project was founded to more than 98 percent in 2007 (Huang, 2009). For the sake of the cost-saving benefits, localization strategy is being adopted by increasing number of automobile FIEs. Honda Fit produced by Guangzhou Honda, a joint venture between Guangzhou Auto Group and Japanese Honda, had 10 percent price cut in 2006 as a result of its rising domestic content ratio from 60 to 80 percent over the past one year. Beijing Hyundai, the manufacturer of Elantra, lowered the price of Elantra 1.6L by 14,000 *yuan* in 2006 when its domestic content ratio increased from 77 to 86 percent.

Even luxury car models whose production has heavily depended on imported parts also participated in the strategic switch toward localization because of the competition pressures for cost-saving measures and lower prices. When the joint venture of First Auto-Volkswagen quickly raised the overall domestic content of Audi A4 series from the negligible level in 2003 to 50 percent in 2005, the price range between the cheaper Audi A4 1.8T on one extreme and more expensive Audo A4 3.0 Quattro on the other shifted downward from 379,000–559,000 to 275,400–475,900 *yuan*. Mazda 6, a passenger car of the First Auto-Mazda joint venture, refreshed its original domestic content ratio of 40 percent in 2003 with its latest record of 75 percent attained in 2007. In accordance with the rising domestic content, the price of Mazda6 2.3L dropped from 265,800 to 205,000 *yuan* within just 4 years (Liu, 2007).

Rather than an outcome of China's domestic regulations, the rising domestic content of inputs largely resulted from the independent strategic initiatives of the manufacturers. The fact that this pattern emerged well before April 2005, the effective date of Chinese policies against imported auto parts became effective,[3]

---

3 According to the Administrative Rules on Importation of Automobile Parts Characterized as Complete Vehicles (GAC and NDRC, 2005), imported auto parts will be considered to be automobile parts characterized as complete vehicles and assessed a tariff based on the whole vehicle rate, typically 25 per cent, much higher than the 10 percent rate for regular parts, if a sufficient number of imported assemblies are used in manufacturing

suggests localized supplies of inputs, instead of a short-term measure taken by FIEs to comply with China's industrial policies, is a long-term strategy of the automobile FIEs to control their production costs and improve their competitiveness in the market. As illustrated above, most automobile FIEs have already been embedded in a local clustering of suppliers as early as in the 1990s. The domestic supplies of most auto parts did not change even when those policies affecting imports of automobile parts were terminated as a result of arbitration by World Trade Organization (WTO, 2008). Although Huanchen-BMW, a joint venture founded in 2003 and noted for its production of luxury cars, have a currently low domestic content of inputs, they responded to the WTO's arbitration by reaffirming their strategy of localization (Qian 2008).

The pattern of localization as presented above allows us to get a quantitative estimate of the domestic content ratios of FIEs in telecommunication and transportation equipments industries. In 2007, the overall domestic content of inputs was 84.8 percent for all automobile firms in China (Bai Nian Chuang Jing Enterprise Management Consulting Corporation, 2008) and the ratio of outputs produced by FIEs to those produced by the other auto firms was 38 to 62 (China Association of Automobile Manufacturers, 2005). Realistically assume FIEs are more capital-intensive than domestic ones. Given output value is the sum of intermediate inputs and added value derived from labor, that means the ratio of inputs used by FIEs to those by the other firms will be greater than that output ratio. Suppose it was 45 to 55 and the domestic content of inputs for non-FIEs was as high as 80 percent. Then automobile FIEs should have a domestic content of 91 percent so that the overall domestic content ratio could reach 84.8 percent.

It is not a surprise that automobile FIEs had a higher domestic content of inputs than their Chinese peers because many of the latter had to import technology-intensive auto parts such as engines and transmissions while FIEs might localize their production. As stated before, assume the domestic content ratios of FIEs in other manufacturing sectors were no less than it was in the automobile industry. That meant the gap between domestic intermediate inputs used by all manufacturing FIEs and those of SOEs, private firms or collective firms would be even wider. The correlation coefficients between domestic intermediate inputs and multiplier coefficients, however, would not be significantly different from those presented in Table 4.8 as long as the domestic content ratios did not vary

---

the vehicle. Specifically, imported parts will be automobile parts characterized as complete vehicles if any of the following three tests are met: (1) from 1 April 2005, when complete Complete Knocked Down (CKD) or Semi-Knocked Down (SKD) kits are imported to assemble a vehicle; (2) from 1 April 2005, when the vehicle body and engine assemblies, or either of the two main assemblies as well as three or more other assemblies of transmission assembly, drive axle assembly, non-drive axle assembly, vehicle frame assembly, steering system, braking system, or five or more assemblies other than the main assemblies are imported to assemble a vehicle; (3) from 1 July 2008, when the aggregate price of imported parts reaches 60 per cent or more of the price of all parts used in a vehicle.

greatly across industries. Under all these conditions that were not unrealistic, the qualitatively stronger backward linkages and quantitatively greater magnitude of domestic inputs associated with manufacturing FIEs made them a more appealing option than domestic firms would be for municipal governments in China that were hungry for inward investments but had increasingly finite land resources to offer. That concludes the demand-side story underlying the soaring FDI inflows observed from the beginning of this century.

Chapter 5
Representations of Entrepreneurial Urban Growth across Regions in China

The dynamics of FDI in China, as presented at the beginning of this book through "investment index" and "size index," is largely an outcome of entrepreneurial strategies motivated by the fiscal and political systems and maneuvered by localities to expedite urban economic and physical growth. Particularly, local states faced with the impending fiscal reform in the early 1990s and a number of insolvent SOEs at that time turned to FIEs capitalized by FDI as a new engine to boost their revenue prospects, which gave rise to the first wave of soaring FDI inflows. When urban housing and land use reform were initiated in the late 1990s, the representation of local state entrepreneurialism could be typically observed on the scale of municipalities that were the de facto owners of most, if not all, urban land. Municipal tactics to drive up prices of land used for residential and commercial development on the one hand and grant LURs of land for manufacturing production at exceedingly low rates on the other entailed the demand for more efficient use of finite land resource and preference for FDI that is deemed superior to domestic ones in this regard. That is the broader picture underlying the second wave of FDI inflows and improved average size of projects in this century.

The rapid growth of urban real estate and manufacturing sectors achieved on the basis of such entrepreneurialism land use strategies, however, did not have uniform representations across all places in China, a country characterized by considerable regional disparities. Following illustration of the institutional foundation, policy implementation and impacts on FDI dynamics of local state entrepreneurialism in the previous chapters, this chapter will demonstrate the varying extent to which that general logic of entrepreneurial urban growth is applied in eastern, middle and western regions of China, which in turn gave rise to the uneven spatial distribution of FDI. It will also present the increasingly entrepreneurial orientations to generate urban growth by demonstrating the dynamics of urban land prices in hinterland Chinese cities over time.

5.1 Logic of Entrepreneurial Urban Growth

As elaborated through previous chapters of this book, the entrepreneurial urban growth arose from the broader political economic context of China. The centralized Chinese political system forced local states to be engaged in intense competition for short-term tangible accomplishments. The fiscal system institutionalized in 1994 that significantly improved the central share of tax revenues and shifted greater expenditure responsibilities to local governments urged localities to mobilize their revenue collections from manufacturing and real estate. It is under such political economic circumstances that local states took advantage of the market-oriented urban housing and land use reforms initiated in the late 1990s to effectively promote the urban real estate development and attract inward manufacturing investment. Municipalities on the one hand fueled the rise of land prices with controlled land supply for residential and commercial development, while on the other offered land to manufacturing investors at exceedingly low rates.

Furthermore, the growth dynamics of real estate development and manufacturing production not only generated immediate urban physical and economic output but also reinforced each other (see Figure 5.1). First of all, more inward manufacturing investments helped improve the overall value of urban land further. According to urban economic theories, urban land prices are determined by the willingness to pay for its use rights in the competitive land market. Since most employees of manufacturing firms in China are local residents, and commuting between home and work would be costly, land area around manufacturing projects sites would become more valuable with increasing demand for these finite spaces, which would eventually raise the overall urban land prices. Next, increasingly valuable urban land resulting from inward manufacturing investments could be translated into a booming real estate market that would generate a great deal of land granting premium as well as tax revenues. As demonstrated before, those municipal revenues, especially tremendous land granting premium, were usually used to finance urban construction projects such as infrastructure building or sports and tourism facilities.

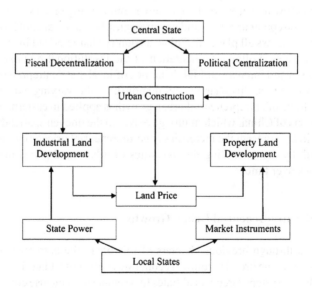

Figure 5.1   Logic of entrepreneurial urban growth in China

Lastly, real estate development as well as urban infrastructure construction not only produced a shaper city image that was usually an important indicator of local economic performance and the achievement of local political leaders, but also facilitated the cost-saving efforts made by manufacturing firms and even generated immediate demand for manufactured goods such as steel and machinery (Zhang, 2002), which in turn stimulated the growth of local manufacturing industries.

5.2 Regional Variation of Local State Entrepreneurialism

The nature of the growth coalition composed of local states, manufacturer investors and real estate developers, however, varied from place to place. In contrast to coastal regions that financed a larger portion of their public expenditures through their own efforts to mobilize revenue collection, the heavy dependence of hinterland regions on central-to-local transfer payments not only indicated the less entrepreneurial orientation of local states in middle and western China, but also suggested a less significant role urban land use played in promoting local economic growth.

5.2.1 Fiscal Patterns and Local State Entrepreneurialism

As mentioned in Chapter 2, a substantial portion of the local budgetary revenues were transfer payments from the central government. In order to measure the independent fiscal strength of local governments, a useful indicator is the ratio of budgetary revenues that were locally generated to total budgetary revenues including transfer payments. A higher such ratio means harder budget constraint and stronger motivation to raise revenues on their own, and vice versa. Table 5.1 shows the ratios were highest for east China and lowest in the west. That is to say, localities in hinterland China were generally much more dependent on the central transfer payment and less motivated to mobilize revenue collection than their peers in the coastal regions.

Local states in eastern, middle and western regions of China not only demonstrated a distinct composition of revenue sources, they also differed from one another with regard to expenditure patterns with those in the east spending the highest proportion of their budget on items associated with business development and urban construction. In Table 5.2, the item of innovation funds and science and technology funds refers to government grants that are used to encourage research and development conducted by enterprises. Although some localities used those funds as tax rebates to attract prospective investors, that switch also reflected the entrepreneurial orientations of local governments to achieve rapid economic growth. So were local budgetary expenditures on urban construction and maintenance. From 2002 to 2006, the eastern region had the most intensive expenditures in these two categories, while middle and western regions spent more on agricultural production and government administration, which was not only a literation representation of the weights of agricultural economy and administrative

Table 5.1   Ratios of locally generated budgetary revenues to local total budgetary revenues, 2002–2006 (%)

		2002	2003	2004	2005	2006
East	Max (Beijing)	78.0	76.2	78.6	82.3	83.0
	Min (Hainan)	48.7	45.2	42.8	44.1	43.9
	All	67.8	68.0	66.9	72.6	73.2
Middle	Max	47.2 (Henan)	46.3 (Henan)	46.9 (Shanxi)	53.4 (Shanxi)	59.1 (Shanxi)
	Min (Jilin)	35.2	34.4	32.1	33.2	34.6
	All	43.2	43.6	42.1	43.9	44.2
West	Max	46.2 (Guangxi)	46.1 (Guangxi)	45.8 (Chongqing)	49.1 (Chongqing)	48.6 (Chongqing)
	Min (Tibet)	5.3	5.8	6.9	5.9	6.6
	All	36.0	38.1	36.6	38.6	38.9

Source: *Finance Yearbook of China*, various years.

Table 5.2   Proportions of local budgetary expenditures in local total budgetary expenditures, 2002–2006 (%)

		2002	2003	2004	2005	2006
Innovation funds & science and technology funds	East	6.80	6.45	6.40	6.21	5.98
	Middle	2.87	4.36	3.25	3.31	2.96
	West	3.38	3.10	2.70	3.89	2.42
Urban maintenance and construction	East	5.55	5.45	5.89	6.23	6.36
	Middle	3.26	3.39	3.48	3.80	3.68
	West	2.87	3.32	3.47	3.70	3.88
Agricultural production	East	5.22	5.13	5.28	5.13	5.09
	Middle	7.06	6.06	8.27	7.12	6.83
	West	8.09	6.90	11.40	8.85	8.79
Government administration	East	8.34	8.75	8.93	8.83	8.91
	Central	9.80	10.03	9.83	9.97	9.51
	West	10.54	11.01	11.09	10.88	10.36

Source: *Finance Yearbook of China*, various years.

system in hinterland China, but also reflected the less entrepreneurial orientations of local states in those regions.

The structure of local public revenues and expenditures as presented above reveals different local governance patterns across regions in China. The greater fiscal independence and more business-oriented efforts made by local governments in the east suggested stronger coalition among the local governments, real estate developers and manufacturers in the east, while the heavier dependence on transfer payments and more intensive expenditures on non-productive government sectors indicated local states in hinterland region were more inclined to maintain the status quo. That is also consistent with the survey-based empirical study by Liu and Tao (2006). They found that local officials in the east usually attached greater importance to their own policy initiatives to build more competitive local investment environment than to those issued by the central government. In contrast, those in western China were mainly concerned with implementing state mandatory regulations regarding birth control, agricultural production and compulsory education.

In addition to the pattern of budgetary revenues and expenditures, different sizes of extra-budgetary funds is another important source of local revenues also mirrored in the behavioral features of local states in east, middle and west China. Because the extra-budgetary funds mainly consist of a great variety of governmental fees and charges, the ratio of extra-budgetary funds to budgetary revenue as presented in Table 5.3 sheds some light on the financial burdens imposed by the local governments on market activities within their jurisdictions. The ratio has been consistently higher in the middle region than it was in the east and west. That distinguishes the relatively more intervening local states in central China from the maintaining ones as identified on the basis of dichotomy between coastal and hinterland regions. In other words, local states in the east, middle and west China were respectively concerned with substantive accomplishment, government interventions and maintaining the *status quo* in a relative sense.

Table 5.3   **Ratios of extra-budgetary funds to local budgetary revenues, 2002–2006 (%)**

	2002	**2003**	**2004**	**2005**	**2006**
East	44.5	40.1	35.3	31.5	31.3
Middle	**56.2**	**49.6**	**44.6**	**41.6**	**35.0**
West	48.6	43.9	35.7	38.4	33.8

Source: *Finance Yearbook of China*, various years.

5.2.2 Dynamics of Urban Land Prices

The differing natures of local states as presented above would become more manifest if we look at how they could maneuver the land-based strategies to achieve entrepreneurial urban growth, or the price dynamics of urban land used for real estate development on the one hand and manufacturing production on the other. Table 5.4 shows the average urban land prices determined through market-based tender, auction and quotation (columns headed by "M") as well as those determined through private negotiations (columns headed by "N") across eastern, middle and western regions.

First of all, the market prices of land in the east were much higher than those in the hinterland on a systematic basis. For example, the market-based prices of land in these regions were 10.6, 4.9 and 6.8 million *yuan* per hectare in 2006 respectively. Secondly, gaps between negotiated land prices in different regions were much smaller than those between market prices. In 2006, the average negotiated prices in those three regions were 1.5, 1.2 and 1.3 million *yuan* per hectare respectively. The prices in the west had been even higher than those in the middle China between 2003 and 2006. Finally, as an indicator of municipal efforts to achieve growth by simultaneously driving up prices of land for real estate development and manipulating the prices of land for manufacturing investments at low rates, the ratios of market-based prices to the negotiated ones were also the highest in the east. They were 3.9, 2.9 and 1.7 in the east, middle and west China in 2003 while 7.1, 4.1 and 5.2 in 2006 respectively.

Table 5.4   Urban land prices across regions in China, 2003–2006 (in million *yuan*/ha.)

	2003		2004		2005		2006	
	M	**N**	**M**	**N**	**M**	**N**	**M**	**N**
East	7.0	1.8	9.2	2.5	9.5	1.6	10.6	1.5
Middle	4.1	1.4	4.4	1.5	5.0	1.4	4.9	1.2
West	2.9	1.7	4.2	2.0	4.8	1.6	6.8	1.3

Note: The columns of "M" are prices determined through market-based mechanisms and those of "N" are negotiation-based prices.
Source: *China Land and Resources Almanac*, various years.

A similar pattern of land prices was also observed at selected cities. Table 5.5 presents the median prices of urban land used for commercial, residential and manufacturing purposes at 31 cities among which 12 were in the east, 8 were in the middle region and 11 were in the west.[1] Most of them are either centrally administered municipalities or the capital cities of the provinces they belong to. Just like the pattern identified on the scale of province, prices of land for commercial or residential development in eastern cities were significantly higher than those in the hinterland ones. In 2006, the median price of land for commercial uses was 30.1 million *yuan* per hectare across 12 eastern cities, nearly 80 percent higher than that in the middle and western cities. So were the land prices for residential development that were 20.5, 13.0 and 10.9 million *yuan* per hectare for the eastern, middle and western cities respectively.

On the other hand, gaps between the prices of land used for manufacturing production in the east and those in the hinterland were not as wide as they were between the prices of land for commercial or residential development. For example, the median price of 5.6 million *yuan* per hectare across the eastern cities in 2006 was only 36 percent higher than that in the west, which is much smaller than the 80 percent gap between the prices of land used for real estate development in these two regions. That meant the prices of land for commercial or residential development in the eastern cities were disproportionally high while those for manufacturing production were exceedingly low, which clearly presented stronger entrepreneurial orientations of local states in the coastal areas than those in the broader hinterland regions.

Table 5.5 Median prices of urban land for commercial, residential and manufacturing uses in 31 major Chinese cities, 2002–2006 (in million *yuan*/ha.)

		2002	2003	2004	2005	2006
Commercial	East	22.0	22.9	24.4	27.4	30.1
	Middle	11.9	12.0	13.9	15.1	16.5
	West	15.2	16.2	16.1	17.0	17.0
Residential	East	12.7	12.8	14.5	17.1	20.5
	Middle	8.9	9.2	10.3	11.7	13.0
	West	8.2	9.2	9.7	10.5	10.9
Manufacturing	East	4.7	5.1	5.2	5.3	5.6
	Middle	3.4	3.6	3.7	3.9	4.3
	West	4.2	4.3	4.0	4.0	4.1

Source: Instant Information System of Urban Land Price in China.

---

1 The 12 eastern cities are Nanjing, Hangzhou, Shanghai, Fuzhou, Guangzhou, Shenzhen, Haikou, Beijing, Tianjin, Shijiazhuang, Jinan and Shenyang. The 8 central cities are Nanchang, Wuhan, Taiyuan, Zhengzhou, Changsha, Hefei, Changchun, Haerbin. The 11 western cities are Xian, Chongqing, Chengdu, Guiyang, Kunming, Nanning, Wulumuqi, Xining, Lanzhou, Yinchuan, Huhehaote.

This regional variation of local state entrepreneurialism also implied that real estate development and manufacturing production played a much bigger role in local economic growth in the east than they did in the hinterland. In 2006, the combined fixed asset investments in these two sectors across cities in the east amounted to be 72 percent of the total, while that proportion in middle and western cities was merely 49 and 39 percent respectively (SSB, 2007a). For a country whose economic growth had been largely driven by fixed asset investments, that suggested that real estate and manufacturing was more significant to local economic performances in the east than it was to hinterland regions. Furthermore, the growth of the real estate sector and manufacturing reinforced each other via large-scale urban construction that usually has to be financed by land granting premium collected from real estate development. Table 5.6 shows that land granting premium in the east reached 542.0 billion *yuan* in 2006, approximately half of their total budgetary revenues and substantially higher than those of the hinterland regions.

That not only meant more extensive urban construction in the east than in the middle and west China, but also suggested stronger stimulating effects generated in local manufacturing industries.

Table 5.6   Gross land granting premium in eastern, central and western regions of China, 2002–2006

		2002	**2003**	**2004**	**2005**	**2006**
Gross land granting premium (in billion *yuan*)	East	185.23	408.66	445.84	398.76	541.97
	Middle	36.24	72.02	99.59	96.99	135.32
	West	20.21	61.45	95.79	92.63	130.47
Gross land granting premium / local budgetary revenues (%)	East	33.9	64.3%	59.8%	41.4%	46.5%
	Middle	22.3	39.0%	44.2%	34.8%	37.8%
	West	14.1	37.3%	48.3%	37.6%	42.6%

Source: China Land and Resources Almanac, various years.

5.2.3 Implications for Manufacturing Land Use

The faster growth of manufacturing and real estate in the east as a result of the stronger local state entrepreneurialism made land a tighter constraint for urban development in that region (Sun, 2005) and led to higher costs associated with granting LURs to manufacturing investors at low rates, which encouraged municipalities there to improve land use efficiency. Many existing projects with less intensive land use patterns are being advised by local governments in east or middle China to move elsewhere in order to make room for projects that are expected to be more productive on unit acreage of land (Jiang, 2008). The spatial-economic outcome of this transformation was the more efficient urban land use in the east than that in the hinterland region. Table 5.7 presents the range of standardized ratios of fixed asset investments, tax revenues and GDP to total land areas across 32 major national EDTZs with a full score of 10. The average indices of the 20 eastern EDTZs were significantly higher than those of their counterparts in the middle and western regions. The two EDTZs at Shanghai had the highest indices while that of Wuhan (next only to Nanchang with regard to GDP) and Chengdu (next only to Huhehaote with regard to tax revenues) took the lead in middle and west China respectively.

Table 5.7   Indices of land use efficiency at national ETDZs, 2006

		Fixed asset investments	Tax revenues	GDP
East	Max	10 (Shanghai Hongqiao)	10 (Shanghai Minhang)	10 (Shanghai Hongqiao)
	Min	0.81 (Shenyang)	0.39 (Qingdao)	0.30 (Qingdao)
	Overall	**1.58**	**2.12**	**1.27**
Middle	Max	1.41 (Wuhan)	2.09 (Wuhan)	1.33 (Nanchang)
	Min (Taiyuan)	0.24	0.17	0.06
	Overall	**0.83**	**1.05**	**0.67**
West	Max	1.41 (Chengdu)	0.79 (Huhehaote)	0.65 (Chengdu)
	Min (Xi'an)	0.80	0.44	0.42
	Overall	**0.89**	**0.56**	**0.41**

Source: China Development Zone Yearbook, 2007.

Beyond the boundaries of ETDZs, intensive land use pattern in the east was also reflected by heavier concentration of FDI in that region. The "investment index" of FDI in each province of China as shown in Table 5.8 was reported in US\$/100 *yuan* because the numerator and denominator were counted in US\$ and Chinese *yuan* respectively. For example, the index of 1.01 for Beijing in 2003 meant 1.01 US\$ utilized FDI among every 100 *yuan* of total fixed asset investment. For each year between 2003 and 2006, the coastal region had the highest attainment of 1.41, 1.29, 1.30 and 1.31 respectively, which was immediately followed by

middle provinces with the indices of 0.50, 0.44, 0.51 and 0.43. Western areas
were ranked the third with the lowest "investment indices" of 0.16, 0.13, 0.24
and 0.24. Although these indices were computed on the basis of aggregate FDI
statistics, manufacturing FDI at a few places for which data was available also
demonstrated a similar pattern of distribution. For example, the investment index
of FDI in manufacturing sector was 2.69 US$ per 100 *yuan* for coastal province of
Zhejiang in 2005, while as low as 0.27 for the middle provinces of Shanxi. Such
regional disparities remain intact in 2006 when that index was 2.28, 0.31 and 0.04
for Zhejiang, Shanxi and Gansu respectively (SSB, various years-a).

**Table 5.8   The "investment indices" of provinces, 2003–2006 (in US$/100
yuan)**

		2003	2004	2005	2006
East	Max	2.19 (Shanghai)	2.07 (Shanghai)	2.23 (Tianjin)	2.40 (Tianjin)
	Min (Hebei)	0.39	0.22	0.46	0.44
	Overall	**1.41**	**1.29**	**1.30**	**1.31**
Middle	Max (Jiangxi)	1.24	1.19	1.11	1.05
	Min (Shanxi)	0.19	0.06	0.15	0.21
	Overall	**0.50**	**0.44**	**0.51**	**0.43**
West	Max	0.45 (Guangxi)	0.24 (Guangxi)	0.45 (Inner Mongolia)	0.52 (Inner Mongolia)
	Min	0.02 (Xinjiang)	0.03 (Xinjiang)	0.02 (Gansu)	0.03 (Gansu)
	Overall	**0.16**	**0.13**	**0.24**	**0.24**

Source: *China Statistical Yearbook, China Commerce Yearbook, China Foreign Economic
Statistical Yearbook*, various years.

5.3 Rise of Entrepreneurial Local States in Hinterland China

To say urban physical and economic growth was faster in east China does not
mean that no growth at all was achieved in the hinterland. Rather, local states in
the middle and west regions are demonstrating their increasingly entrepreneurial
orientations over time. The financial burden of fees and charges imposed by
localities on enterprises and individuals were alleviated to a considerable extent.

Those in the middle region that were conventionally characterized by their intervening actions made the greatest efforts in this regard. As shown in Table 5.3, their ratio of extra-budgetary funds to the locally generated revenues shrank from 56.2 to 35 percent from 2002 to 2006. In the meantime, local states in hinterland regions also increased their public expenditures on urban construction that was critical to promote the mutually reinforcing urban real estate development and economic growth. Table 5.2 shows its proportion in local total budgetary expenditures rose from 3.26 to 3.68 percent and from 2.87 to 3.88 percent in middle and west China respectively. As a result of all these measures, fiscal independence of local states in hinterland regions as measured by the ratio of locally generated budgetary revenues to total budgetary revenues increased between 2004 and 2006 even though their improvements were less than that in the east (see Table 5.1).

The rising local state entrepreneurialism in the hinterland region was also reflected by the dynamics of urban land prices there. Although it is shown in Table 5.4 that eastern cities have the highest market-based prices of land, the unparalleled rate of growth occurred in the west where the average land prices as determined through tender, auction and quotation rocketed from 2.9 to 6.8 million *yuan* per hectare in just three years. Table 5.9 presents the price range of land for residential, commercial and manufacturing purposes at 15 major cities in hinterland China. The average residential and commercial land prices increased by 35 percent between 2002 and 2006, which meant an annual growth rate of nearly 8 percent. In the meantime, land market transactions in hinterland regions were booming too. In 2003, the acreage of land with LURs granted to developers was 10,660 and 9,862 hectares in middle and west China respectively, but rocketed to 14,075 and 12,655 hectares in 2005 (MLR, various years). As a result of the rising land prices and booming land transactions, land granting premium collected by local states in hinterland regions expanded (see Table 5.6) and tax revenues generated by real estate sector in the middle and west China increased from 7.34 and 8.94 billion *yuan* in 2003 to 24.51 and 24.78 billion *yuan* in 2006 respectively (NTB, various years).

The increasingly stronger local state entrepreneurialism in hinterland China can also be observed through the dynamics of land used for manufacturing production. The land price grew at a much slower rate than those for residential and commercial land uses. From 2002 to 2006, average manufacturing land prices increased by 15 percent at the 19 major hinterland cities (see Table 5.9) at an annual rate below 3 percent, which was much less than the 8 percent annual rate for prices of land used for commercial or residential development. On the other hand, the acreage of land with LURs granted to manufacturing investors kept increasing, which mirrored the influx of manufacturing investments in hinterland regions. For example, there were 21,288 and 19,272 hectares of land in middle and west China respectively whose LURs were granted via negotiation to investors in 2003. The figures rapidly rose to 31,238 and 26,944 in 2006. Given that a majority of the negotiations were conducted between municipalities and prospective manufacturing investors, the growing acreage of land use reflected substantial growth of inward manufacturing investments in hinterland China. Between 2003 and 2006, for instance, the weight of fixed asset investments in manufacturing sector among total fixed asset investments rose from 18.2 to 19.3 percent in the west and from 25.9 to 29.0 in the middle region (SSB, various years). If the dynamics of land prices in hinterland China indicated the entrepreneurial efforts of the local states to expedite local economic growth, the effect can be confirmed by that achievement.

Table 5.9   Average urban land prices at hinterland cities, 2002–2006 (in *yuan* per square meter)

		2002	2003	2004	2005	2006
R	Max	1,122 (Chongqing)	1,261 (Chongqing)	1,332 (Chongqing)	1,801 (Chengdu)	2,020 (Chengdu)
	Min (Huhehaote)	627	641	665	671	701
	Average	890	855	970	1,113	1,199
C	Max	2,707 (Chengdu)	3,003 (Chengdu)	3,344 (Chengdu)	4,538 (Guiyang)	4,720 (Guiyang)
	Min	912 (Nanchang)	946 (Zhengzhou)	1,103 (Zhengzhou)	1,041 (Hefei)	1,058 (Hefei)
	Average	1,424	1,493	1,648	1,812	1,923
M	Max (Wuhan)	602	630	629	645	654
	Min (Nanchang)	230	237	257	273	280
	Average	392	400	437	431	452

Note: R, C, M denote the prices of land for residential, commercial and manufacturing uses respectively.

Source: Instant Information System of Urban Land Price in China.

Conclusions:
Toward Sustainable Urban Development

The impacts of local state entrepreneurialism are well beyond the dynamics FDI as identified at the beginning of this book. Pervasive FIEs capitalized by FDI in manufacturing industries generated astonishing export performance as well as pressure for Chinese currency appreciation that became the target of speculative capital. Soaring urban property values resulting from the booming urban real estate sector also motivated the cross-border mobility of capital to make quick profits. Starting from a discussion of such "hot money" and the complication it caused to FDI, the inquiry of this book, this section will assess the sustainability of entrepreneurial urban growth in China and conclude with direction of future reforms.

"Hot Money": Consequence of Extensive FDI and Local State Entrepreneurialism

Since China started its foreign exchange rate reform in July 2005, the magnitude of FDI that goes to manufacturing industries indeed has been debated because some of the inflows were reported to be used for speculation on Chinese currency appreciation or urban real estate properties. Named "hot money", such cross-border capital inflows are not intended to acquire a "lasting interest" in the direct investment enterprise, by holding no less than 10 per cent of the ordinary shares or voting power. Rather, they aim to seek short-term super-profits by taking advantage of asset prices such as a favorable exchange rate or soaring real estate values in the destination country. FDI then becomes one of the channels through which "hot money" enters China where strict capital account regulations make the entry, convertibility and exit of such capital flow difficult.[1]

Despite there being no agreement on its specific size, the presence of such "hot money" not only provides an additional piece of evidence for the extensive presence of FDI in China, it also reflects the entrepreneurial orientations of Chinese local states that are highly concerned with the quantitative growth of local economies. Firstly, to a large extent, the appreciation pressure of Chinese currency results

---

1   Other important channels include trade and underground banking. "Hot money" enters when the export prices are inflated and import prices are deflated in trade activities between affiliated firms across borders. Underground banking, on the other hand, is to illegally convert foreign capital into domestic currency.

from tremendous export volume of manufactured goods in China, a majority of which were produced by FIEs (see Table I.1).[2] Although it had been debated how much exchange rate of Chinese currency deviated from its real value, both camps unanimously related the pressure for appreciation to the export performance of China. Currency appreciation was either deemed as the political response of developed countries to the competitive export-oriented industries of China (Lin, 2007) or as the strategy China should adopt to rebalance its own economic growth and make it less dependent on investment and export (Lu, 2006). In other words, Chinese currency may not be pressed to appreciate or "hot money" may not be a concern if manufacturing FDI were not as pervasive in China as identified in the first chapter of this book.

Next, entry of "hot money" into China in the appearance of FDI was also facilitated by entrepreneurial Chinese local states that would like to achieve a high record of FDI inflows. For example, the requests by existing manufacturing FIEs to increase their investments could be approved with such ease that some of that added capital was eventually used to finance the purchase of exchange stocks or real estate properties instead of machinery and equipment (Zhou, 2008). The exclusive focus of local states on the statistics of FDI inflows within their jurisdictions alerted the central government that was concerned with the impact of "hot money" on the Chinese economy. In July 2006, the Ministry of Construction and other five central state agencies including MOC, NDRC, PBC, State Administration for Industry and Commerce (SAIC), and State Administration of Foreign Exchange (SAFE), jointly promulgated the Opinions on Regulating the Entry into and the Administration of Foreign Investment in the Real Estate Market that explicitly required FIE be institutionally established before any real estate transactions can be conducted (MOF, MOC et al. 2006).

The restriction against speculation of "hot money" on domestic real properties was further reinforced by a few other regulatory government documents that aimed to supervise cross-border investments more closely. According to the Circular on Reinforcing and Standardizing the Examination, Approval and Regulation of FDI in Real Estate issued on 5 August 2007, local governments must file all newly approved FIEs engaged in real estate development with the Ministry of Commerce (MOC and SAFE, 2007). On 31 October, the amended Guiding Catalogue on Industries for Foreign Investment added secondary real estate market as a sector where FDI would be subject to restriction (NDRC and MOC, 2007). In July 2008, the NDRC issued the Circular on Improving and Regulating the Management of Foreign Invested Projects in order to prevent the deviation of FDI from their intended purposes (NDRC 2008).

---

2   For an overview of the exchange rate policy of China, see Goldstein and Lardy (2008).

Misaligned Central-Local Relationship

The entry of "hot money" in the appearance of FDI is just one illustration of the effects caused by local state entrepreneurialism across Chinese cities. Other cases include municipal hospitalities toward projects capitalized by foreign investments without adequate evaluation of their impacts on environment and public health or minimum concerns with the workfare conditions. It is not uncommon to witness that quite a few cities intensely compete for a prospective manufacturing project with their respective packages of preferential treatment in which LURs granting is an essential component. As previous chapters have demonstrated, the prices of land for manufacturing production were driven increasingly downward. Although the central state promulgated the Circular on the Promulgation and Implementation of the National Minimum Pricing Standards for Manufacturing Land that explicitly sets minimum prices of manufacturing land for all cities in China (MLR, 2006), the real prices could still be as low as negative in some places if ad hoc refund by municipalities to investors was taken into account. Free land use that was prevalent in Chinese cities before 1980 recurred in the inter-urban competition for manufacturing investments.

The ubiquitous manipulation of urban land use by Chinese local states to boost urban physical and economic growth is an outcome of local reactions to the shift of fiscal and land use institutions. The fiscal system before 1994 both encouraged and enabled localities to achieve GDP growth without rising budgetary revenue. The tactics of "concealing revenue" as facilitated by extra-budgetary funds led to the declining ratios of budgetary revenue to GDP and central budgetary revenue to the national total, which prompted the central state to set up separate central taxation agencies responsible for the collection of both central and shared taxes. As that conventional approach built upon the tacit mutual agreement between local states and SOEs was no longer needed or effective under the tax assignment system of 1994, inward investment became an indispensable factor to generate economic growth and municipal revenue. It is in this context that the reforms of urban housing provision and land use were eventually transformed by the local states to drive up the prices of land for real estate development on the one hand and grant LURs to manufacturing investors at excessively low rates on the other.

The reforms of both fiscal and land use systems were initially launched by the central state to address issues of national significance, which, however, were largely beyond the concerns of localities. The fiscal reform in 1994 aimed to strengthen local budgetary management and consolidate the central financial strength, while that of land use and housing reforms in the late 1990s was to substitute a market-based pricing mechanism for socialist welfare distribution in order to achieve more efficient urban land use and housing provision. The implementation by the local states in practice, however, generated consequences that were largely unintended by central decision-makers. The fiscal reform stimulated the local states to host inward investment, especially FDI, at the expense of improving the strength of domestic firms, the consequence of which was that municipalities usually undervalued the equity contribution of local SOEs in order to form joint ventures with prospective foreign investors, a practice known as "fire sales" of state assets (Fu, 1998). On the other hand, considerable prospects of local revenue generation associated with real estate development and manufacturing production not only motivate municipalities to affect prices of land used for these purposes but also lead to the relentless acquisition of arable land without just compensation to rural farmers.

At the root of these local strategic actions, or the misaligned interests between the central and local states, is the centralized political system of China. The excessive concerns of local states with short-term economic growth, for instance, were largely mandated by the performance-based evaluation system of local officials. Their efforts to achieve tangible performance were unchecked by substantive accountability to the constituents within the jurisdictions. Without improved accountability or a new system of cadre evaluation, the only policy solution to problems associated with local state entrepreneurialism would be for the central state to put brakes on ambitious local initiatives. For example, in order to keep localities from granting LURs to manufacturing investors at exceedingly low rates, the MLR issued the Circular on Relevant Issues Concerning the Implementation of the Land Use System for Manufacturing Production by Means of Tender, Auction and Quotation that put an end to LURs granted via private negotiation to manufacturing investors from June 30 2007 (MLR, 2007).

From Quantitative Entrepreneurial Growth to Qualitative Sustainable Development

Despite tangible achievements it generates, the rapid urban physical and economic growth in China driven by land development can hardly be sustained in the long run. First of all, the effect of residential land development on economic growth will be fading away as market-based housing provision gradually deviates from its social function (UN Millennium Project, 2005). In 2000, the price of a regular urban housing unit was equivalent to 6.3 times of the annual disposable income of an urban household.[3] That ratio rose to 7.2 in 2006 and were even as high as 11.5 and 12.1 in 2005 at Beijing and Shanghai respectively, which suggested urban housing was less affordable for prospective homeowners and least for those living in major cities (SSB, 2007). As the gap between urban housing prices and household incomes became wider, housing development and purchases were increasingly driven by speculative capital instead of demand for residence, which has already led to excess inventory or may even end up with the bubble bursting.

---

3   The formula used to compute this ratio is $(P \times M \times N)/(I \times N)$, where P, M, I and N denotes the average housing price in *yuan* per square meter floor area, the average housing floor area per capita, the average disposable income per capita and the average number of heads per household respectively.

For example, the nationwide floor area of vacant urban residential units grew from 57.7 million square meters at the end of November 2007 to 70.8 million square meters in just one year (SSB, 2007). It reached 5.2 million square meters at the city of Beijing by the end of 2008.

The heavy dependence of municipal revenue on real estate development and the increasing amount of speculative capital in housing production and consumption exposed rapid urban growth in China to risks associated with domestic policy shift and international economic fluctuations. As mentioned before, the soaring urban property prices attracted the attention of international "hot money." Its entry not only pushed the prices further up but also contributed to China's domestic inflation. In order to cool down the investment fervor, China's central bank consecutively raised the deposit reserve ratio of commercial banks for five times from 14.5 to 17.5 percent in the first half of 2008. That was expected to reduce capital supply to many real estate developers who had been depending on bank loans to launch land development projects. The condition was further aggravated by the international financial crisis breaking out in the second half of that year. Land prices plummeted and the number of developers became fewer. As a result, both the land granting premium and the tax revenue collected from real estate sector substantially shrank (Zhao and Chen 2008; Ruan 2009), which prompted many municipal policies to encourage housing purchases (China News Service 2008).

Secondly, the municipal objectivity to attract inward manufacturing investments especially FDI is usually achieved at the expense of Chinese domestic industrial development. As mentioned above, the tremendous aggregate export volume in which nearly 60 percent was contributed by FIEs put China under the pressure of its currency appreciation. Since the exchange rate reform in 2005, however, Chinese currency appreciation generated asymmetric impacts on export-oriented domestic firms and FIEs. Because the former as a whole (not in a specific sector such as telecommunication or automobile where the condition could be the reverse) may have higher domestic content of input, they would be less able to take advantage of the appreciated Chinese currency to import input materials from abroad. More importantly, Chinese domestic manufacturing firms are generally more vulnerable to the impact of currency appreciation on their export performances than FIEs. Many of their products are labor-intensive ones that have lower added value and can be easily substituted by those manufactured by their competitors in other countries. In a roundabout way, the hunger of Chinese local states for FDI aggravated the predicament of Chinese domestic firms through export boost and currency appreciation.

Finally, even to the extent that spillover effects of manufacturing FDI help improve the productivities of domestic peers, few empirical studies lend support to the notion this process would occur spontaneously and unanimously. Rather, it is conditional upon a range of socioeconomic factors in which major efforts by the local governments to "embed" the FIE is a critical one (Wang 2001; Wang and Lin 2007). Unfortunately, partly due to the exclusive municipal concern with quantitative growth and partly due to the corporate strategy of FIEs, the domestic rivals of FIEs did not benefit from the spillover effects as well as their subordinate domestic suppliers did. That has also been confirmed by numerous empirical findings that the spillover effects of FDI on improving high-end technology of domestic firms were much less significant than on low-end technology (Fan and Warr, 2000; Bennett, Liu et al. 2001; Zhang and Taylor 2001; Cheng 2003; Ping, Guan et al. 2007).

All these consequences arising from the underlying local state entrepreneurialism or more intermediate FDI hunger entail further reforms to realign the center-local relationship and achieve more sustainable urban and national development.[4] In the short run, ambitious local land use plans need to be immediately fixed. One important measure is to rebalance the asymmetric power relations between prospective investors and farmers by initiating land use reform in rural areas and encouraging alternative uses of arable land in a more productive and sustainable way. On the intermediate level, local fiscal starvation that motivates entrepreneurial urban growth has to be addressed. Local expenditure responsibilities should be met by corresponding revenue sources to relieve the quest for economic growth at all costs. One option is to raise the share of institutionalized general-purpose transfers in total center-to-local transfer payments so that local public service provision can be equalized across places. More fundamentally, the centralized system of administrative evaluation and political appointment for government officials that drives the inter-urban competition for tangible economic performance awaits significant improvements with regard to its accountabilities to local constituencies. Reforms in these aspects may not only mitigate the dependence of urban economic and physical growth on land use, but also would shift the present pattern of growth toward a qualitatively more sustainable path of development where the intensive use of innovative knowledge takes the place of extensive input of material resources as the driver of the Chinese economy. At that time, FDI inflows would demonstrate their new role in economic development of China.

---

4   Lardy (2007) identified six factors that prompted the rethinking of China's investment-dependent growth strategy by its decision makers. They are: (1) the over investment and excess capacity resulting from the investment driven growth led to less efficient use of resources; (2) a more consumption driven growth path may alleviate or at least slow the pace of increasing income inequality; (3) the investment driven growth has generated very modest gains in employment; (4) the burgeoning energy consumption and its detrimental effects on the environment associated with investment driven growth; (5) rising non-performing loans in the banking system as a result of the excess investment in some sectors; (6) reliance on net export raises the prospect of a protectionist backlash in the United States and other countries.

Appendix 1

Official Foreign Exchange Rates in Chinese Currency (Median Prices)

Table A.1   **Official foreign exchange rates in Chinese currency (median prices)**

Year	100 US Dollars	100 Japanese Yen	100 HK Dollars	100 Euros
1993	576.20	5.2020	74.41	–
1994	861.87	8.4370	111.53	–
1995	835.10	8.9225	107.96	–
1996	831.42	7.6352	107.51	–
1997	828.98	6.8600	107.09	–
1998	827.91	6.3488	106.88	–
1999	827.83	7.2932	106.66	–
2000	827.84	7.6864	106.18	–
2001	827.70	6.8075	106.08	–
2002	827.70	6.6237	106.07	800.58
2003	827.70	7.1466	106.24	936.13
2004	827.68	7.6552	106.23	1,029.00
2005	819.17	7.4484	105.30	1,019.53
2006	797.18	6.8570	102.62	1,001.90

Note: Euro entered into circulation in 2002.

Source: *China Statistical Yearbook*, 2007.

Appendix 2

Computation of Backward Linkage Index

The backward linkage indices of a certain industry can be computed from an input-output table. The initial effort should be attributed to Rasmussen (1956), who applied the Leontief inverse matrix $(I - A)^{-1}$ to the mathematical measurement of linkage effects. Formally, the backward linkage index is specified as the column summation of Leontief inverse matrix which is computed on the basis of the input–output table. More specifically, suppose the whole economy consists of n sectors and sectors sell and buy from one another. Apart from being used as intermediate input in the other sectors, the products of each sector also go to satisfy the final demand such as export, consumption and asset formation. On the other hand, each sector also derives a portion of their input, or value added, from sources beyond the inter-sectoral relationship such as labor, fixed assets and so on. This input–output interaction can be represented by Table 5.6, where X_{ij} is the production volume (usually in monetary units) of sector i that goes to sector j as intermediate inputs, E_{qj} is the production of external input source q that is acquired by sector j, and D_{ip} is the final demand of category p for the products of sector i whose total inputs/outputs is Y_i.

Table A.2   Input–output framework

Output / Input		Intermediate output (X)						Final Demand (D)			Total Output (Y)
		1	2	...	j	...	n	1	...	p	
Inter-mediate Input (X)	1	X_{11}	X_{12}	...	X_{1j}	...	X_{1n}	D_{11}	...	D_{1p}	Y_1
	2	X_{21}	X_{22}	...	X_{2j}	...	X_{2n}	D_{21}	...	D_{2p}	Y_2
	:										
	i	X_{i1}	X_{i2}	...	X_{ij}	...	X_{in}	D_{i1}	...	D_{ip}	Y_i
	:										
	n	X_{n1}	X_{n2}	...	X_{nj}	...	X_{nn}	D_{n1}	...	D_{np}	Y_n
External Input (I)	1	E_{11}	E_{12}	...	E_{1j}	...	E_{1n}				
	:										
	q	E_{q1}	E_{q2}		E_{qj}		E_{qn}				
Total Input (Y)		Y_1	Y_2		Y_j		Y_n				

It is then clear that:

$$Y_i = X_{i1} + X_{i2} + \cdots + X_{in} + \sum_j D_{ij} = X_{1i} + X_{2i} + \cdots + X_{ni} + \sum_j E_{ji} \quad (1)$$

Keep in mind we are interested in the backward rather than forward linkage with the purpose to measure the increase in the total output of the economy triggered by the increase of final demand in a sector. We then focus on the first half of equation that is:

$$Y_i = X_{i1} + X_{i2} + \cdots + X_{in} + \sum_j D_{ij} \quad (2)$$

and make the assumption that the ratio of X_{ij} to Y_j is a constant under a certain level of technology. In other words, it is plausibly assumed that demands of sector j for the intermediate inputs produced by all sectors are proportional to its total input. Thus, equation (2) can be rewritten as:

$$Y_i = a_{i1}Y_i + a_{i2}Y_i + \cdots + a_{in}Y_i + \sum_j D_{ij}$$

or in matrix notation:

$$Y = AY + D \quad (3)$$

where Y and D are the column vector of total inputs and aggregate final demand respectively,

$$A = \begin{bmatrix} a_{11} & a_{12} & \cdots & a_{1j} & \cdots & a_{1n} \\ a_{21} & a_{22} & \cdots & a_{2j} & \cdots & a_{2n} \\ \cdots & \cdots & \cdots & \cdots & \cdots & \cdots \\ a_{i1} & a_{i2} & \cdots & a_{ij} & \cdots & a_{in} \\ \cdots & \cdots & \cdots & \cdots & \cdots & \cdots \\ a_{n1} & a_{n2} & \cdots & a_{nj} & \cdots & a_{nn} \end{bmatrix}, \text{ and } a_{ij} = X_{ij}/Y_j$$

Now, the solution value of Y is given by $Y = (I - A)^{-1}D$ where I is an n by n identity matrix and $(I - A)^{-1}$ is the Leontief inverse matrix. Denoting the total increase in the output of the economy as a response to the one unit of increase in final demand of the jth sector, the backward linkage effect can be captured by

$$M_j = \sum_i r_{ij} \quad (4)$$

in which r_{ij} is the element located on the ith row and jth column of the Leontief inverse matrix.

In order to get a better sense of the relative strength of linkages across sectors, the multiplier coefficient is usually compared with the overall average multiplier for the economy as a whole, a way resembling the calculation of location quotient in regional analysis. Mathematically, it is specified as:

$$R_j = \frac{\sum_j r_{ij}}{\sum_{ij} r_{ij} / n} \tag{5}$$

The numerator of equation (5) is the multiplier coefficient of sector j while the denominator is the average multiplier coefficient for all n sectors. Thus, sectors whose relative index R_j is higher than 1 are supposed to be focused on by policy makers because the increase in final demand in those sectors will yield above average linkage effects.

References

Agarwala, R. 1992. *China: reforming intergovernmental fiscal relations*. Washington, DC: World Bank.

Ahmad, E., Li, K., Richardson, T. and Singhl, R. 2002. Recentralization in China? *IMF Working Paper 02/168*. Washington, DC: IMF.

Bai Nian Chuang Jing Enterprise Management Consulting Corporation. 2008. *Analysis and Investment Consulting Report of Automobile Sector in China (zhongguo qi che hang ye fen xi ji tou zi zi xun bao gao)*. Shenzhen.

Bardhan, P. 2002. Decentralization of governance and development. *Journal of Economic Perspectives* 16(4): 185–205.

Bennett, D., Liu, X. and Parker, D. 2001. Technology transfer to China: a study of strategy in 20 EU industrial companies. *International Journal of Technology Management* 21(1/2): 151–182.

Bertaud, A. and Renaud, B. 1992. Cities without land markets. *World Bank Discussion Paper 227*, Washington, DC: World Bank.

Blanchard, O. and Shleifer, A. 2000. Fiscal federalism with and without political centralization: China versus Russia. *NBER Working Paper No. 7616*, Cambridge, MA: The National Bureau of Economic Research.

Broadman, H. and Sun, X. 1997. The distribution of foreign direct investment in China. *World Economy* 20(3): 339–361.

Buckley, P. and Casson, M. 1985. *The Economic Theory of the Multinational Enterprises*. New York, St. Martin's Press.

Caves, R. 1974. Multinational firms, competition, and productivity in host-country markets. *Economica* 41(162): 176–193.

Caves, R.E. 2007. *Multinational Enterprise and Economic Analysis*. Cambridge: Cambridge University Press.

CCP Central Committee (CCPCC). 1956. *Opinions on the Basic Conditions of Current Urban Private Property and Its Socialist Transformation (guan yu mu qian cheng shi si you fang chan ji ben qing kuang ji jing xing she hui zhu yi gai zao de yi jian)*. Beijing.

CCP Central Committee (CCPCC). 1992. *Opinions on Expediting Reform, Opening Wider to the Outside World, and Working Harder to Raise the Economy to a Higher Level in a Better and Faster Way (zhong gong zhong yang guan yu jia kuai gai ge, kuo da kai fang, li zheng jing ji geng hao geng kuai de shang yi ge xin tai jie de yi jian)*. Beijing.

CCP Central Committee (CCPCC). 1993. *Decision on Issues Regarding the Establishment of a Socialist Market Economic System (zhong gong zhong yang guan yu jian li she hui zhu yi shi chang jing ji ti zhi ruo gan wen ti de jue ding)*. Beijing.

Central People's Government. 1950. *Land Reform Act of People's Republic of China* (*zhong hua ren min gong he guo tu di gai ge fa*). Beijing.

Chandler, A. 1977. *The Visible Hand: The Managerial Revolution in American Business*. Cambridge, MA: Belknap Press.

Chan, N. 1999. Land-use rights in mainland China: problems and recommendations for improvement. *Journal of Real Estate Literature* 7(1): 53–63.

Chang, H.-J. 2002. *Kicking Away the Ladder: Development Strategy in Historical Perspective*. London: Anthem.

Chen, C.-H. 1996. Regional determinants of foreign direct investment in mainland China. *Journal of Economic Studies* 23(2): 18–30.

Chen, C., Chang, L. and Zhang, Y. 1995. The role of foreign direct investment in China's post-1978 economic development. *World Development* 23 (4): 691–703.

Chen, G., Gu, C., and Wu, F. 2006. Urban poverty in the transitional economy: a case of Nanjing, China. *Habitat International* 30 (1): 1–26.

Chen, X. 2001. Chongqing Ericsson announced 2 billion purchases of supplies (Chongqing Ericsson fang chu er shi yi cai gou ju dan). *The 21st Century Business Herald* (*er shi yi shi ji jing ji bao dao*), 30 October.

Chen, Y. 2003. The interdependence between Motorola and its Chinese suppliers: cooperation and "win-win" situation (ni zhong you wo,wo zhong you ni: Motorola yu zhongguo gong ying shang de he zuo he shuang ying). *FDI in China* (*zhongguo wai zi*), 12 (5): 22–23.

Chen, Z. 2008a. How big is the government (zheng fu gui mo you duo da)? *Economic Observer News* (*jing ji guan cha bao*). 25 February, 42.

Chen, Z. 2008b. Why does income growth lag behind that of GDP (wei shen me bai xing shou ru gan bu shang GDP zeng zhang)? *Nanfang Weekend* (*nan fang zhou mo*). 7 August, 32.

Chenery, H.B. and Clark, P.G. 1959. *Interindustry Economics*. New York: Wiley.

Cheng, L. and Kwan, Y. 2000. What are the determinants of the location of foreign direct investment? The Chinese experience. *Journal of International Economics* 51(2): 379–400.

Cheng, S. 1999. *Reforms of China's Urban Housing System: Objectives and Implementations* (*zhongguo cheng zhen zhu fang zhi du gai ge: mu biao mo shi yu shi shi nan dian*). Beijing: Democracy and Construction Press (min zhu yu jian she chu ban she).

Cheng, Y. 2003. Technology spillovers via FDI in China (FDI dui zhongguo de ji shu yi chu xiao ying yan jiu). Master of Economics Thesis, School of Economics, Zhejiang University. Hangzhou.

China Association of Automobile Manufacturers. 2005. *China Automative Industry Yearbook* (*zhongguo qi che gong ye nian jian*). Beijing: China Machinery Industry Press (zhongguo ji xie gong ye chu ban she).

China Association of Development Zones. 2007. *China Development Zone Yearbook* (*zhongguo kai fa qu nian jian*). Beijing: China Finance and Economics Press (zhongguo cai zheng jing ji chu ban she).

China Banking Regulatory Commission (CBRC). 2007. *Report on the Opening-up of the Chinese Banking Sector* (*zhongguo yin hang ye dui wai kai fang bao gao*). [Online]. Available at: http://www.cbrc.gov.cn/chinese/home/jsp/docView.jsp?docID=20070322E53EB19A80F47157FFF41FBA56F2E700 [accessed: 10 September 2009].

China Central Television (CCTV). 2007a. *Expose the Office Buildings in Violation Against State Regulations* (*qing li dang zheng ji guan wei gui lou*). [Onine]. Available at: http://news.cctv.com/china/20070923/102528.shtml [accessed: 6 June 2008].

China Central Television (CCTV). 2007b. *Stop the Wicked Ethos of Building Luxurious Office Buildings (sha zhu jian hao hua ban gong lou wai feng)*. [Onine]. Available at: http://news.cctv.com/special/C18662/index.shtml [accessed: 6 June 2008].

China Central Television (CCTV). 2008. *Solutions to the Issue of Land Acquisition* (*zheng di po ju*). [Online]. Available at: http://v.cctv.com/html/xinwendiaocha/2008/11/xinwendiaocha_300_20081122_1.shtml [accessed: 22 November 2008].

China News Service (CNS). 2008. *16 Municipal Governments Take Actions to Boost Real Estate Market, New National Policies are Impending* (*quan guo 16 cheng shi di fang zheng fu chu zhao jiu lou shi, lou shi xin zheng huo chu tai*). [Onine]. Available at: http://www.chinanews.com.cn/estate/gdls/news/2008/10-16/1415022.shtml [accessed: 11 February 2009].

China Securities Regulatory Commission (CSRC). 2006. *Circular on Issues Relevant to the Implementation of "QFII Management Measures"* (*guan yu shi shi "QFII guan li ban fa" you guan wen ti de tong zhi*). Beijing.

Chung, J.H. (Ed.). 1999. *Cities in China: Recipes for Economic Development in the Reform Era*. London: Routledge.

Coase, R. 1937. The nature of the firm. *Economica* 4(16): 386–405.

Deng, X. 1980. *Talk on Urban Housing Issues*. [Online]. Available at: http://news.xinhuanet.com/book/2007-11/06/content_7020046.htm [accessed: 20 March 2009].

Duckett, J. 1998. *The Entrepreneurial State in China: Real Estate and Commerce Departments in Reform Era Tianjin*. London: Routledge.

Dunning, J. 1980. Toward an eclectic theory of international production: some empirical tests. *Journal of International Economic Studies* 11(1): 9–31.

Dunning, J. 1995. Re-appraising the eclectic paradigm in an age of alliance capitalism. *Journal of International Economic Studies* 26(3): 461–91.

Edin, M. 2003. State capacity and local agent control in China: CCP cadre management from a township perspective. *China Quarterly* 173: 17–34.

Fan, X. and Warr, P. 2000. Foreign investment, spillover effects and the technological gap: evidence from China. *Working Paper in Trade and Development No. 00/03*. Canberra, Australia: Australian National University.

Fletcher, K. 2002. *Tax Incentives in Cambodia, Lao PDR, and Vietnam.* IMF Conference on Foreign Direct Investment: Opportunities and Challenges for Cambodia, Lao PDR and Vietnam, Hanoi, Vietnam, 16–17 August 2002.

Florida, R.L. 2002. *The Rise of the Creative Class: And How It's Transforming Work, Leisure, Community and Everyday Life.* New York: Basic Books.

Florida, R.L. 2005. *The Flight of the Creative Class: the New Global Competition for Talent.* New York: Harper Business.

Fong, P.K.W. 1988. *Housing Reforms in China: Privatization of Public Housing in a Socialist Economy.* The 5th CAP Plenary Conference and Southeast Asia Workshop, Hong Kong, 28 November –3 December 1988.

Fitzgerald, J. 2002. *Rethinking China's Provinces.* London: Routledge.

Fu, J. 2000. *Institutions and investments: foreign direct investment in China during an era of reforms.* Ann Arbor: University of Michigan Press.

General Administration of Customs, National Development and Reform Commission, et al. 2005. *Administrative Rules on Importation of Automobile Parts Characterized as Complete Vehicles (gou cheng zheng che te zheng de qi che ling bu jian jin kou guan li ban fa).* Beijing.

Gereffi, G. and Bonacich, E. 1994. Power and profits in the apparel commodity chain, in *Global Production: the Apparel Industry in the Pacific Rim*, edited by E. Bonacich. Philadelphia: Temple University Press: 42–62.

Gereffi, G., Humphery, J. and Sturgeon, T. 2005. The governance of global value chains. *Review of International Political Economy* 12(1): 78–104.

Goldstein, M. and Lardy, N.R. (Eds). 2008. *Debating China's Exchange Rate Policy.* Washington, DC: Peterson Institute for International Economics.

Gong, H.M. 1995. Spatial patterns of foreign investment in China's cities. *Urban Geography* 16(3): 189–209.

Graham, E. and Wada, E. 2001. Foreign direct investment in China: effects on growth and economic performance. *Peterson Institute Working Paper Series No. WP01–3.* Washington, DC: Peterson Institute.

Guo, Y. 2008. Li Jinhua points out the problem of "zhu jing ban" (Li Jinhua zhi chu "zhu jing ban" wen ti zheng jie). *Jinghua Times (jing hua shi bao).* 11 March, 8.

Hall, T. and Hubbard, P. 1996. The entrepreneurial city: new urban politics, new urban geographies. *Progress in Human Geography* 20(2): 153–174.

Harvey, D. 1989. From managerialism to entrepreneurialism: the transformation in urban governance in late capitalism. *Geografiska Annaler. Series B, Human Geography* 71(1): 3–17.

He, C. 2005. *Location of Foreign Direct Investment: Theoretical Analysis and Empirical Studies (wai shang zhi jie tou zi qu wei: li lun fen xi yu shi zheng yan jiu).* Beijing: China Economy Publishing House (zhongguo jing ji chu ban she).

Head, K. and Ries, J. 1996. Inter-city competition for foreign investment: static and dynamic effects of China's incentive areas. *Journal of Urban Economics* 40(1): 38–60.

Hendrischke, H. and Feng, C. 1999. *The Political Economy of China's Provinces: Comparative and Competitive Advantage.* London: Routledge.

Hirschman, A. 1958. *Strategy of Economic Development.* New Haven: Yale University Press.

Ho, S.P.S. and Lin, G.C.S. 2003. Emerging land markets in rural and urban China: policies and practices. *China Quarterly* 105: 681–707.

Hou, J. and Zhang, K. 2001. A locational analysis of Taiwanese manufacturing branch plants in mainland China. *International Journal of Business* 6(2): 53–66.

Huang, S. 2009. Santana can not be priced at 50 thousand yuan (sang ta na bu ke neng jiang zhi 5 wan yuan). *China Youth Daily (zhongguo qing nian bao).* 12 February, 9.

Huang, Y. 2003. *Selling China: Foreign Direct Investment During the Reform Era.* New York: Cambridge University Press.

Hymer, S. 1976. *The International Operations of National Firms: A Study of Direct Foreign Investment.* Cambridge, M.: MIT Press.

International Monetary Fund. 2008. *Balance of Payments and International Investment Position Manual (6th Edition).* [Onine]. Available at: http://www.imf.org/external/pubs/ft/bop/2007/pdf/BPM6.pdf [accessed: 10 March 2009].

Jessop, B. and Sum, N.-L. 2000. An entrepreneurial city in action: Hong Kong's emerging strategies in and for (inter)urban competition. *Urban Studies* 37 (12): 2287–2313.

Jia, K. and Liu, J. 2007. *Studies on Housing Reforms in China: Solution to "ju zhe youqi wu" in a Transitional Economy (zhongguo zhu fang zhi du gai ge wen ti yan jiu: jing ji she hui zhuan gui zhong "ju zhe you qi wu" de qiu jie).* Beijing: Economic Science Press (jing ji ke xue chu ban she).

Jiang, F., Christodoulou, C. and Wei, H.-C. 2001. The determinants of international pharmaceutical firms' FDI in China: a comparison between early (pre-1992) and late (from-1992) entrants. *Management Decision* 39(1): 45–56.

Jiang, X. 2006. New stage of China's opening up: integration into the global economy in more balanced approach (zhongguo dui wai kai fang jin ru xin jie duan: geng jun heng he li de rong ru quan qiu jing ji). *Economic Research Journal (jing ji yan jiu)* 41(3): 4–14.

Jiang, M. 2008. Increasingly robust metropolitan Wuhan (da Wuhan geng jia jie shi ting bao). *Hubei Daily (Hubei ri bao).* 3 September, 9.

Jin, J. and Zou, H. 2003. Soft-budget constraint on local governments in China, in *Fiscal Decentralization and the Challenge of Hard Budget Constraints,* edited by J. Rodden, G.S. Eskeland and J. Litvak. Cambridge, MA: MIT Press, 289–324.

Jin, J. and Zou, H. 2005. Fiscal decentralization, revenue and expenditure assignments, and growth in China. *Journal of Asian Economics* 16(6): 1047–1064.

Kindleberger, C. 1969. *American Business Abroad: Six Lectures on Direct Investment.* New Haven: Yale University Press.

Kornai, J. 1990. The affinity between ownership forms and coordination mechanisms: the common experience of reform in socialist countries. *Journal of Economic Perspectives* 4(3): 131–147.

Krugman, P. 1991. *Geography and Trade*. Cambridge, MA: MIT Press.

Kwok, Y.W. 1986. *Urban Housing Provision in China After 1978*. World Planning and Housing Congress, Adelaide, Australia, 28 September–3 October 1986.

Lall, S. 1997. *Learning From the Asian Tigers: Studies in Technology and Industrial Policy*. New York: St. Martin's Press.

Lall, S. 2000. FDI and development: policy and research issues in the emerging context. *Queen Elizabeth House Working Paper Series: No. 43*, Oxford: Oxford University.

Lall, S. and Narula R. 2004. FDI and its role in economic development: Do we need a new agenda? *MERIT-Infonomics Research Memorandum Series*: *No. 19*. Maastricht: Maastricht Economic Research Institute on Innovation and Technology.

Lardy, N. 1975. Centralization and decentralization in China's fiscal management. *China Quarterly* 61: 25–60.

Lardy, N. 1994. *China in the World Economy*. Washington, DC: Institute for International Economics.

Lardy, N. 2007. *China: Rebalancing Economic Growth*. China Balance Sheet in 2007 and Beyond, Washington, DC, 2 May.

Lardy, N. 2008. Sustaining Economic Growth in China, in *China's Rise: Challenges and Opportunities*, edited by C. Bergsten, C. Freeman, N.R. Lardy and D. Mitchell. Washington, DC: Peterson Institute for International Economics: 105–137.

Leontief, W.W. 1941. *The Structure of American Economy, 1919–1929: An Empirical Application of Equilibrium Analysis*. Cambridge, MA: Harvard University Press.

Leontief, W.W. 1966. *Input-Output Economics*. New York: Oxford University Press.

Li, H. and Zhou, L.-A. 2005. Political turnover and economic performance: the incentive role of personnel control in China. *Journal of Public Economics* 89(9–10): 1743–1762.

Li, L.-H. 1999. *Urban land reform in China*. New York: St. Martin's Press.

Li, W. 2008. Come back to the origin (zhuan le ge quan er you hui dao qi dian)? *Vision Globalization Discernment (jing ji dao kan)* 7(4): 71.

Lieberthal, K. 1995. A new China strategy: the challenge. *Foreign Affairs* 74(6): 35–49.

Lieberthal, K. 1997. China's governing system and its impacts on environmental policy implementation. *China Environmental Series 1*. Washington, DC: The Woodrow Wilson International Center for Scholars.

Lin, Y. 2007. Rethinking the issue of RMB appreciation and its policy implications (guan yu ren min bi hui lv wen ti de si kao yu zheng ce jian yi). *Working*

Papers Series C2007001. Beijing: China Center for Economic Research, Peking University.

Lin, Y. and Liu, Z. 2000. Fiscal decentralization and economic growth of China (zhongguo de cai zheng fen quan yu jing ji zeng zhang). *Working Paper Series C2000008*. Beijing: China Center for Economic Research, Peking University.

Liu, M. and Tao, R. 2006. *Local Governance, Policy Mandates and Fiscal Reform in China*. [Onine]. Available at: http://jlin.ccer.edu.cn/article/article. asp?id=336 [accessed: 6 October 2008].

Liu, X. 2007. Car prices leveraged by domestic contents of inputs. (guo chan hua lv qiao dong che jia). *Beijing Morning Post (Beijing chen bao)*. 26 June, 25.

Liu, X., Song, H., Wei, Y. and Romilly, P. 1997. Country characteristics and foreign direct investment in China: A panel data analysis. *Review of World Economics (Weltwirtschaftliches Archiv)* 133(2): 313–329.

Liu, Y. and Wu, F. 2006. Urban poverty neighbourhoods: typology and spatial concentration under China's market transition, a case study of Nanjing. *Geoforum* 37(4): 610–626.

Lu, F. 2006. The implications of over 1 trillion foreign exchange reserves (wai hui chu bei guo wai yi mei yuan de shen ceng gen yuan yu ren shi qi shi). *Working Papers Series C2006021*. Beijing: China Center for Economic Research, Peking University.

Luo, Y. 1997. Pioneering in China: Risks and benefits. *Long Range Planning* 30(5): 768–776.

Ma, J. and Norregaard, J. 2000. *China's Fiscal Decentralization*. Agenda for Sequencing Decentralization in Indonesia, Jakarta, Indonesia, 20–21 March 2000.

Ma, K. 1992. *China Reform Encyclopedia 1978–1991: Volume of Land System Reform (zhongguo gai ge quan shu 1978–1991: tu di zhi du gai ge juan)*. Dalian: Dalian Press.

Markusen, A. 1996. Sticky places in slippery space: A typology of industrial districts. *Economic Geography* 72(3): 293–313.

Ministry of Commerce (MOC), various years. *China Commerce Yearbook. (zhongguo shang wu nian jian)*. Beijing: China Commerce and Trade Press.

Ministry of Commerce (MOC) and State Administration of Foreign Exchange (SAFE). 2007. Circular on Reinforcing and Standardizing the Examination, Approval and Regulation of FDI in Real Estate (guan yu jin yi bu jiang qiang, gui fan wai shang zhi jie tou zi fang di chan shen pi he jian guan de tong zhi). Beijing.

Ministry of Construction. 2002–2005. *Urban Construction Yearbook of China (zhongguo cheng shi jian she nian jian)*. Beijing: China Architecture and Building Press (zhongguo jian zhu gong ye chu ban she).

Ministry of Finance (MOF). 1992a. *Accounting Standards for Business Enterprises (qi ye kuai ji zhun ze)*. Beijing.

Ministry of Finance (MOF). 1992b. *General Rules on Enterprise Finance (qi ye cai wu tong ze)*. Beijing.

Ministry of Finance (MOF), various years. *Finance Yearbook of China (zhongguo cai zheng nian jian)*. Beijing: China Finance Press (zhongguo cai zheng za zhi she).

Ministry of Finance (MOF), Ministry of Commerce (MOC), et al. 2006. *Opinions on Regulating the Entry into and the Administration of Foreign Investment in the Real Estate Market (guan yu gui fan fang di chan shi chang wai zi zhun ru he guan li de yi jian)*. Beijing.

Ministry of Foreign Trade and Economic Cooperation, various years. *Almanac of China's Foreign Economic Relations and Trade (zhongguo dui wai jing ji mao yi tong ji nian jian)*. Beijing: Foreign Trade and Economic Press (zhongguo dui wai jing ji mao yi chuban she).

Ministry of Land and Resources (MLR). 2002. *Regulations on Granting Land Use Rights via Tender, Auction and Quotation (zhao biao pai mai gua pai chu rang guo you tu di shi yong quan gui ding)*. Beijing.

Ministry of Land and Resources (MLR). 2004. *Circular on Continuing the Supervision over Granting Land Use Rights for Commercial Development via Tender, Auction and Quotation (guan yu ji xu kai zhan jing ying xing tu di shi yong quan zhao biao pai mai gua pai chu rang qing kuang zhi fa jian cha gong zuo de tong zhi)*. Beijing.

Ministry of Land and Resources (MLR). 2004. *Guidelines on Improving the Compensation and Settlement associated with Land Acquisition (guan yu wan shan zheng di bu chang an zhi zhi du de zhi dao yi jian)*. Beijing.

Ministry of Land and Resources (MLR). 2006 *Circular on the Promulgation and Implementation of the "National Minimum Pricing Standards for Manufacturing Land" (guan yu fa bu shi shi "quan guo gong ye yong di chu rang zui di jia" de tong zhi)*. Beijing

Ministry of Land and Resources (MLR). 2007. *Circular on Relevant Issues Concerning the Implementation of the Land Use System for Manufacturing Production by Means of Tender, Auction and Quotation (guan yu luo shi gong ye yong di zhao biao pai mai gua pai chu rang zhi du you guan wen ti de tong zhi)*. Beijing.

Ministry of Land and Resources (MLR). 2008. *Instant Information System of Urban Land Price in China (zhongguo cheng shi di jia dong tai jian ce xi tong)*. [Onine]. Available at: http://www.landvalue.com.cn [accessed: 20 September 2008].

Ministry of Land and Resources (MLR), various years. *China Land and Resources Almanac (zhongguo guo tu zi yuan nian jian)*. Beijing: China Land Press (zhongguo da di chu ban she).

Municipal Government of Beijing. 2002. *Regulations Regarding the Termination of Negotiated Land Use Rights Granting for Real Estate Development (guan yu ting zhi jing ying xing xiang mu guo you tu di shi yong quan xie yi chu rang you guan gui ding de tong zhi)*. [Onine]. Available at: http://www.bjgtj.gov.cn/publish/portal0/tab200/info3160.htm [accessed 20 August 2008].

Municipal Government of Beijing. 2004. *Supplementary Regulations on Terminating the Negotiated Land Use Rights Granting for Commercial Development* (*guan yu ting zhi jing ying xing xiang mu guo you tu di shi yong quan xie yi chu rang de bu chong gui ding*). [Onine]. Available at: http://www.bjgtj.gov.cn/publish/portal0/tab200/info3123.htm [accessed 20 August 2008].

National Audit Office of the People's Republic of China (NAO). 2008. *The Audit Investigation Results of the Land Use Rights Granting Premium* (*guo you tu di shi yong quan chu rang jin shen ji diao cha jie guo*). [Onine]. Available at: http://www.audit.gov.cn/n1057/n1072/n1282/1589058.html [accessed 23 August 2008].

National Development and Reform Commission (NDRC) 2008. *Circular on Improving and Regulating the Management of Foreign Invested Projects* (*guan yu jin yi bu jia qiang he gui fan wai shang tou zi xiang mu de tong zhi*). [Onine]. Available at: http://www.sdpc.gov.cn/zcfb/zcfbtz/2008tongzhi/t20080718_226080.htm [accessed 23 August 2008].

National Development and Reform Commission (NDRC) and Ministry of Commerce (MOC) 2007. *Guiding Catalogue on Industries for Foreign Investment* (*wai shang tou zi chan ye zhi dao mu lu*). [Onine]. Available at: http://www.sdpc.gov.cn/zcfb/zcfbl/2007ling/t20071107_171058.htm [accessed 23 August 2008].

National People's Congress (NPC) 1979. *Law of the PRC on Chinese-Foreign Equity Joint Ventures* (*zhong hua ren min gong he guo zhong wai he zi jing ying qi ye fa*). Beijing.

National People's Congress (NPC). 1980. *Income Tax Law of the PRC on Chinese-foreign Equity Joint Ventures China* (*zhong hua ren min gong he guo zhong wai he zi jing ying qi ye suo de shui fa*). Beijing.

National People's Congress (NPC). 1982. *Constitution of the People's Republic of China* (*zhong hua ren min gong he guo xian fa*). Beijing.

National People's Congress (NPC). 1988. *Land Management Law of the PRC* (*zhong hua ren min gong he guo tu di guan li fa*). Beijing.

National People's Congress (NPC). 1991. *Income Tax Law for FIEs of the PRC* (*zhong hua ren min gong he guo wai shang tou zi qi ye he wai guo qi ye suo de shui fa*). Beijing.

National People's Congress (NPC). 1994. *Budget Law of PRC* (*zhong hua ren min gong he guo yu suan fa*). Beijing.

National Taxation Bureau (NTB), various years. *Tax Yearbook of China* (*zhongguo shui wu nian jian*). Beijing: China Taxation Press (zhongguo shui wu chu ban she).

Naughton, B. 1996. China's emergence and prospects as a trading nation. *Brookings Papers in Economic Activity* (2): 273–344.

North, D. 1990. *Institution, Institutional Change, and Economic Performance*. Cambridge: Cambridge University Press.

North, D. 2005. *Understanding the Process of Economic Change*. Princeton: Princeton University Press.

Organisation for Economic Co-operation and Development (OECD). 2008. *OECD Benchmark Definition of Foreign Direct Investment* (4th Edition). [Onine]. Available at: http://www.oecd.org/dataoecd/26/50/40193734.pdf. [accessed 10 March 2009].

Oi, J.C. 1992. Fiscal reform and the economic foundations of local state corporatism. *World Politics* 45(1): 99–126.

Oi, J.C. 1996. The Role of the Local State in China's Transitional Economy, in *China's Transitional Economy*, edited by A.G. Walder. Oxford: Oxford University Press, 170–187.

Oksenberg, M. and Tong, J. 1991. The evolution of central-provincial fiscal relations in China, 1971–1984: the formal system. *China Quarterly* 125: 1–32.

Overholt, W. 2005. China and Globalization. *RAND Corporation Testimony Series CT-244*, Arlington, VA: RAND Corporation.

People's Bank of China (PBC). 1998. *Management Measures on Individual Housing Mortgages* (*ge ren zhu fang dai kuan guan li ban fa*). Beijing.

People's Bank of China (PBC). 2006. *The Implementation Report of China's Monetary Policy in the 4th Quarter of 2006* (*2006 nian di si ji du zhongguo huo bi zheng ce zhi xing bao gao*). Beijing.

People's Congress of Guangdong Province. 1982. *Interim Provisions on Land Management in Shenzhen Special Economic Zone* (*Shenzhen jing ji tu qu tu di guan li zan xing gui ding*). Guangzhou.

Ping, X. 2006. Evaluation of local budgetarary performance in China (zhongguo di fang yu suan ti zhi de ji xiao ping gu ji zhi biao she ji). *Working Paper Series C2006018*. Beijing, China Center for Economic Research, Peking University.

Ping, X., Guan, X., et al. 2007. Market for technology (shi chang huan lai ji shu le ma)? *Working Paper Series C2007004*. Beijing, China Center for Economic Research, Peking University.

Piore, M. and Sabel, C. 1984. *The Second Industrial Divide: Possibilities for Prosperity*. New York: Basic Books.

Po, L.-C. 2003. Making trans-border governance: a case study of the role of Taiwanese capital in Kunshan's institutional change (kua jie zhi li: tai zi can yu kun shan zhi du chuang xin de ge an yan jiu). *Working Paper Series: No. 2003012*. Beijing, China Center for Economic Research, Peking University.

Porter, M.E. 1998. *On Competition*. Boston: Harvard Business School Publishing.

Qian, C. 2008. The arbitration of WTO does not affect the strategy of localization (WTO cai jue bu gai guo chan hua zhan lue). *Dongfang Daily* (*dong fang zao bao*). 15 February, 10.

Qian, Y.-Y. 2006. The process of China's market transition, 1978–1998: the evolutionary, historical and comparative perspectives, in *China's Deep Reform : Domestic Politics in Transition*, edited by L. Dittmer and G. Liu. Lanham, MD: Rowman & Littlefield Publishers.

Qian, Y. and Weingast, B. 1996. China's transition to markets: market-preserving federalism, Chinese style. *Journal of Policy Reform* 1(1): 149–185.

Qian, Y. and Xu, C. 1993. Why China's economic reforms differ: the M-form hierarchy and entry/expansion of the non-state sector. *Economics of Transition* 1(2): 135–170.

Qu, T. and Green, M.B. 1997. *Chinese Foreign Direct Investment: A Subnational Perspective on Location.* Aldershot, UK: Ashgate.

Rasmussen, P. 1956. *Studies in Intersectoral Relations.* Amsterdam: North Holland.

Ren, Z. 2009. *Never Shift Away From "Marketization" ("shi chang hua" de fang xiang bu bian).* [Onine]. Available at: http://blog.sina.com.cn/s/blog_4679d3510100cnnb.html [accessed 18 February 2009].

Riskin, C. 2000. Decentralization in China's transition. *Bratislava Policy Papers #4.* Bratislava, UNDP.

Ruan, Y. 2009. *Total Land Granting Premium of 960 Billion yuan in 2008, Abruptly Declining Land-Based Revenues (08 nian zhongguo tu di chu rang zong shou ru 9600 yi yuan, tu di shou ru rui jian).* [Onine]. Available at: http://www.chinanews.com.cn/cj/gncj/news/2009/01–15/1530151.shtml [accessed 11 February 2009].

Shah, A. and Shen, C. 2006. Reform of the intergovernmental transfer system in China. *World Bank Policy Research Working Paper No. 4100.* Washington, DC: World Bank.

Shanghai Municipal Statistical Bureau. 2008. *Shanghai Statistical Yearbook 2008.* Beijing: China Statistical Press.

Song, X. 1992. *Studies on China's Fiscal System Reform (zhongguo cai zheng ti zhi gai ge yan jiu).* Beijng: China Finance and Economic Publishing House (zhongguo cai zheng jing ji chu ban she).

State Statistical Bureau (SSB). 2003. *China 2002 Input-Output Table (zhongguo 2002 tou ru chan chu biao).* Beijing: China Statistics Press.

State Statistical Bureau (SSB), various years-a. *China Statistical Yearbook (zhongguo tong ji nian jian).* Beijing: China Statistics Press.

State Statistical Bureau (SSB), various years-b. *China Industry Economy Statistical Yearbook (zhongguo gong ye jing ji tong ji nian jian).* Beijing: China Statistics Press.

State Statistical Bureau (SSB), various years-c. *Statistical Yearbook on Investment in Fixed Assets of China (zhongguo gu ding zi chan tou zi nian jian).* Beijing: China Planning Press (zhongguo ji hua chu ban she).

State Statistical Bureau (SSB), various years-d. *China Foreign Economic Statistical Yearbook (zhongguo dui wai jing ji mao yi tong ji nian jian).* Beijing: China Statistics Press.

State Council. 1950. *Suburban Land Reform Ordinance (cheng shi jiao qu tu di gai ge tiao li).* Beijing.

State Council. 1983. *Provisional Regulation Concerning the Tax-for-Profits in SOEs (guan yu guo ying qi ye li-gai-shui shi xing ban fa).* Beijing.

State Council. 1984. *Interim Provisions of the State Council of the PRC on Preferential Tax Treatment at SEZs and 14 COCs (zhong hua ren min gong he guo guo wu yuan guan yu jing ji te qu he 14 ge yan hai gang kou cheng shi jian zheng, mian zheng qi ye suo de shui he gong shang tong yi shui de zan xing gui ding*). Beijing.

State Council. 1988a. *Implementation Plan to Practice Urban Housing System Reform by Stages and in Batches* (*guan yu zai quan guo cheng zhen fen qi fen pi tui xing zhu fang zhi du gai ge de shi shi fang an*). Beijing.

State Council. 1988b. *Tentative Ordinance of PRC on Urban Land Use Tax* (*zhong hua ren min gong he guo cheng zhen tu di shi yong shui zan xing tiao li*) Beijing.

State Council. 1990a. *Interim Measures for the Administration of the Foreign-invested Development and Management of Tracts of Land* (*wai shang tou zi jing ying cheng pian tu di zan xing guan li ban fa*). Beijing.

State Council. 1990b. *Provisional Regulation on Granting and Transferring Land Use Rights of Urban State-Owned Land in Cities and Towns* (*zhong hua ren min gong he guo cheng zhen guo you tu di shi yong quan chu rang he zhuan rang zan xing tiao li*). Beijing.

State Council. 1991. *Circular on Promoting Comprehensive Urban Housing Reform* (*guan yu quan mian tui jin cheng zhen zhu fang zhi du gai ge de tong zhi*). Beijing.

State Council. 1993. *Circular Concerning the Strict Examination and Approval and Checks on Various Development Zones* (*guan yu yan ge shen pi he ren zhen qing li ge lei kai fa qu de tong zhi*) Beijing.

State Council. 1994. *Decision on Deeping Urban Housing System Reform* (*guan yu shen hua cheng zhen zhu fang ti zhi gai ge de jue ding*). Beijing.

State Council. 1996. *Decision on Reinforcing the Management of Extra-budgetary Funds* (*guo wu yuan guan yu jia qiang yu suan wai zi jin guan li de jue ding*) Beijing.

State Council. 1998. *Circular on Further Deepening Urban Housing Reform and Expediting Housing Construction* (*guan yu jin yi bu shen hua cheng zhen zhu fang zhi du gai ge jia kuai zhu fang jian she de tong zhi*). Beijing.

State Council. 2005. *Circular on Effectively Stabilizing Housing Prices* (*guan yu zuo hao wen ding zhu fang jia ge gong zuo de yi jian*). Beijing.

State Council. 2006a. *Opinions about Adjusting Housing Supply Structure to Stabilize Housing Price* (*guan yu tiao zheng zhu fang gong ying jie gou wen ding zhu fang jia ge de tong zhi*) Beijing.

State Council. 2006b. *The Outline of the 11th Five-Year Plan for the Development of National Economic and Social Development of PRC* (*zhong hua ren min gong he guo guo min jing ji he she hui fa zhan di shi yi ge wu nian ji hua gang yao*). Beijing.

State Council. 2007. *Notice about Implementation of Preferential Policies on Transition of Enterprise Income Tax* (*guan yu shi shi qi ye suo de shui guo du you hui zheng ce de tong zhi*) Beijing.

Statistical Bureau of Guangdong Province, various years. *Guangdong Statistical Yearbook* (*guang dong tong ji nian jian*). Beijing: China Statistical Press.

Su, M. and Zhao, Q. 2004. *China's Fiscal Decentralization Reform*, International Symposium on Fiscal Decentralization in Asia Revisited, Tokyo, Japan, 20–21 February 2004.

Sun, Q., Tong, W. and Yu, Q. 2002. Determinants of foreign direct investment across China. *Journal of International Money and Finance* 21(1): 79–113.

Sun, X. 2008. State intervenes in the vicious competition for investments at Yangtze River Delta (guo wu yuan jiao ting chang san jiao e xing zhao shang jing zheng). *21st Century Business Herald*. 25 September, 7.

Tao, R., Lin, Y., Liu, M. and Zhang, Q. 2004. Rural taxation and government regulation in China. *Agricultural Economics* 31(2–3): 161–168.

Thun, E. 1999. Changing lanes in China: industrial development in a transitional economy. *Ph.D. Dissertation at Department of Government*. Cambridge, MA: Harvard University.

United Nations Conference on Trade and Development (UNCTAD). 2000. *World Investment Report 2000: Cross-border Mergers and Acquisitions and Development*. New York and Geneva: United Nations.

United Nations Conference on Trade and Development (UNCTAD). 2008. *Key Data from WIR Annex Tables*. [Onine]. Available at: http://www.unctad.org/Templates/Page.asp?intItemID=3277andlang=1 [accessed 7 October, 2010]

UN Millennium Project. 2005. *A Home in the City*. Task Force on Improving the Lives of Slum Dwellers, lead authors: Garau, P., Sclar, E. and Carolini, G. London: Earthscan.

Vernon, R. 1966. International investment and international trade in the profit life cycle. *Quarterly Journal of Economics* 80(2): 190–207.

Walder, A.G. 1995. Local governments as industrial firms: an organizational analysis of China's transitional economy. *American Journal of Sociology* 101(2): 263–301.

Wang, C. 2006. *The Structure of Housing Financial Market* (*zhu fang jin rong shi chang jie gou*). [Onine]. Available at: http://www.jjxj.com.cn/news_detail.jsp?keyno=10855 [accessed 20 May 2008].

Wang, J. 2001. *Innovative Space: Enterprise Clusters and Regional Development* (*chuang xin de kong jian: qi ye ji qun yu qu yu fa zhan*). Beijing: Peking University Press.

Wang, J. and Lin, T. 2007. New Insights to China's Export-Oriented Clusters. *Acta Scientiarum Naturalium Universitatis Pekinensis* 43(6): 839–846.

Wang, Y.P. and Murie, A. 1999. Commercial housing development in urban China. *Urban Studies* 36 (9): 1475–1494.

Wang, Y.P., Wang, Y.L. and Bramley, G. 2005. Chinese housing reform in state-owned enterprises and its impacts on different social groups. *Urban Studies* 42 (10): 1859–187.

Wei, S. 1995. Attracting foreign direct investment: has China reached its potential? *China Economic Review* 6(2): 187–199.

Wei, Y.D. 2000. *Regional Development in China: States, Globalization, and Inequality*. New York: Routledge.

White, G. 1991. *The Chinese State in the Era of Economic Reform: The Road to Crisis*. London: Macmillan.

Williamson, O. 1975. *Markets and Hierarchies, Analysis and Antitrust Implications: A Study in the Economics of Internal Organization*. New York: Free Press.

Williamson, O. 1981. The modern corporation: origins, evolution, attributes. *Journal of Economic Literature* 19(4): 1537–1568.

Wong, C. 2000. Central-local relations revisited: the 1994 tax-sharing reform and public expenditure management in China. *China Perspectives* 31: 52–63.

Wong, C. 2001. Converting fees into taxes: reform of extra budgetary funds and intergovernmental fiscal relations in China (fei gai shui: zhongguo yu suan wai zi jin he zheng fu jian cai zheng guan xi de gai ge), in *Decentralization of the Socialist State: Intergovernmental Finance in Transition Economies* (*she hui zhu yi guo jia de fen quan hua: zhuan gui jing ji de zheng fu jian cai zheng zhuan yi zhi fu*), edited by R. Bird, R. Ebel and C. Wallich. Beijing: Central Translation Press (zhong yang bian yi chu ban she).

Wong, C.P.W., Heady, C. and Woo, W.T. 1995. *Fiscal Management and Economic Reform in the People's Republic of China*. Hong Kong: Oxford University Press.

Woo-Cumings, M. 1999. *The Developmental State*. Ithaca, NY: Cornell University Press.

World Bank. 2002a. *Global Development Finance 2002: Financing the Poorest Countries*. Washington, DC: World Bank, 41.

World Bank. 2002b. China-national development and sub-national finance: A review of provincial expenditures. *World Bank Report* No. 22951, Washington, DC: World Bank.

World Bank. 2005. *China: Deepening Public Service Unit reform to Improve Service Delievery* (*zhongguo: shen hua shi ye dan wei gai ge, gai shan gong gong fu wu ti gong*). Beijing: Citic Publishing House.

World Trade Organization (WTO). 2008. China-measures affecting imports of automobile parts. *WTO Dispute Settlement 339, 340, 342*. Geneva: WTO.

Wu, F. 1995. Urban processes in the face of China's transition to a socialist market economy. *Environment and Planning C* 13(2): 159–177.

Wu, F. 1996. Changes in the structure of public housign provision in urban China. *Urban Studies* 33(9): 1601–1627.

Wu, F., Xu, J. and Yeh, A. 2007. *Urban Development in Post-Reform China: State, Market, and Space*. London: Routledge.

Wu, J. 2005. *Understanding and Interpreting Chinese Economic Reform*. Mason, OH: Thomson/South-Western.

Wu, W. 1999. *Pioneering Economic Reforms in China's Special Economic Zones: the Promotion of Foreign Investment and Technology Transfer in Shenzhen*. Brookfield: Ashgate.

Xiao, B. and Wang, W. 2007). Fiscal revenues of 260 million *yuan* with more than 100 million spent on the city hall: the extravagence of Gushi in Henan looks incommensurate with its status of impoverished county (cai zheng shou ru liang yi liu, jian zuo da lou yi yi duo: he nan gu shi de pai chang bu tai xiang pin kun xian). *Economic Information Daily (jing ji can kao bao)*, 29 October, 1.

Xiao, G. 2004. People's Republic of China's round-tripping FDI: scale, causes and implications. *Asian Development Bank Institute Discussion Paper: No. 7.* Tokyo, Asian Development Bank Institute.

Xu, S.-J. 2004. The implications of urban grass-root democracy and urban governance in mainland China (zhongguo da lu cheng shi ji ceng ming zhu yu cheng shi zhi li de min zhu hua yi han), in *Studies on the Urban Grass-Root Democracy in Mainland China (zhongguo da lu cheng shi ji ceng min zhu yan jiu)*, edited by X.-M. Zhu. Taibei: Cross-Strait Interflow Prospect Foundation, 109–140.

Yang, C. and Liu, W. 1991. *Economic Studies on China's Real Estate (zhongg guo fang di chan jing ji yan jiu)*. Zhengzhou: Henan People's Publishing House (he nan ren min chu ban she).

Yang, R. 1998. Three-stage model of institutional change in China (wo guo zhi du bian qian zhuan huan de san jie duan lun). *Economic Research Journal (jing ji yan jiu)* 33(1): 3–10.

Ye, M. 2005. *Solution to the Institutional Defects of the Secondary Urban Land Market (cheng shi tu di er ji shi chang de zhi du que xian ji dui ce)*. [Onine]. Available at: http://www.clr.cn/front/read/read.asp?ID=67857 [accessed 12 January 2009].

Yeh, A.G.O. and Wu, F. 1996. New land development process and urban development in Chinese cities. *International Journal of Urban and Regional Research* 20(2): 330–353.

Young, C. and Kaczmarek, S. 1999. Changing the perception of the post-socialist city: place promotion and imagery in Lodz, Poland. *Geographical Journal* 165(2): 183–191.

Yu, B. and Zheng, X. 2003. Cultivated land crisis and blindness in the process of urbanization (geng di wei ji yu cheng shi hua jin cheng de mang mu xing). *Urban Problems (cheng shi wen ti)* 22 (3): 58–60.

Yu, J. 2005. *Why does An Industrial Policy Fail in China?: Political economic analysis on China's Industrial Policy in the Automobile Industry (wei shen me yi ge chan ye zheng ce zai zhongguo hui shi bai?: guan yu zhongguo qi che chan ye zheng ce de zheng zhi jing ji xue fen xi)*. The 5th China Economics Annual Conference, Xiamen, China, 10–11 December 2005.

Zhang, J. and Wu, F. 2006. China's changing economic governance: administrative annexation and the reorganization of local governments in the Yangtze River Delta. *Regional Studies* 40(1): 3–21.

Zhang, T. 2002. Urban development and a socialist pro-growth coalition in Shanghai. *Urban Affairs Review* 37(4): 475–499.

Zhang, W. and Taylor, R. 2001. EU technology transfer to China: the automotive industry as a case study. *Journal of the Asia Pacific Economy* 6(2): 261–274.

Zhang, X. 1997. Urban land reform in China. *Land Use Policy* 14(3): 13.

Zhao, F. and Chen, X. 2008. The crossroad of the "secondary fiscal system" ("di er cai zheng" shi zi lu kou). *The 21st Century Business Herald (er shi yi shi ji jing ji bao dao)*, 3 November, 5

Zheng, C. 2008. Proposal to lift the ban against local debt financing with focus on local capacity to repay (fang xing di fang fa zhai zhengce tai dong, fang di fang zhai wu hei dong cheng jiao dian). *Nanfang Daily (Nanfang ri bao)*. 3 November, 13.

Zhou, C. 2005. What is the lure of paradise for tax avoidance (bi shui tian tang you huo he zai)? *China Territory Today (jin ri guo tu)* 4 (Z4): 37.

Zhou, L. 2007. Study on the championship-based political promotion system of Chinese local officials (zhongguo di fang guan yuan de jin sheng jin biao sai yan jiu). *Economic Research Journal (jing ji yan jiu)* 42(7): 36–50.

Zhou, P. 2008. Intense competition for inward investments may facilitate the entry of hot money (zhao shang yin zi kuang biao tu jin, huo wei re qian kai fang bian zhi men). *Shanghai Securities News (Shanghai zheng quan bao)*. 14 August, 2.

Zhu, H. 2008. Shanghai strongly adjusts the salaries of public employees (Shanghai qiang li tiao zheng gong wu yuan chou xin). *Nanfang Weekend (Nan fang zhou mo)*. 24 April, 10.

Index

All references are to China unless otherwise indicated